Writing from Private Places to Public Spaces

Alice Robertson

Western Illinois University

Second Edition

Kendall Hunt
publishing company

Cover design by Barbara J. Arvin

Cover model: Angela Zaba

Kendall Hunt
publishing company

www.kendallhunt.com
Send all inquiries to:
4050 Westmark Drive
Dubuque, IA 52004-1840

Printed in the United States of America
10 9 8 7 6 5 4 3 2 1

Contents

Acknowledgments

This second edition of the customized text for English 180, Western Illinois University's freshman writing course, is a collaborative product that consists of materials from teaching assistants and instructors as well as my authorial material. While I wrote the introductions, rationales, transitional matter, and two of the three appendices in this text, the majority of the exercises and activities and all the student writing samples were provided by those contributors. Without their vital contributions, advice, and hard work, this text would not exist:

Diana Allen
Michael Bauman
Emily Brackman
Kay Hamada
Shane Hill
William Iavarone
Dave King
Lindsay Miller
Kelly Potter
Julie Veile
Erin Waters
Joe Weinberg
Rebecca Wort

I also wish to acknowledge Joe Weinberg for voluntarily proofreading the final manuscript of the first edition, and the Writing Program secretary, Judi Hardin, for typing and merging the materials into a single text for both editions. But I especially want to thank the two teaching assistants, Emily Brackman and Erin Waters, who worked closely with me on a weekly basis to produce this updated, expanded second edition. They both located and produced additional exercises and helped me to decide what to add and where to add it in this second text. Both deserve considerable credit for the shape and content of the final manuscript. Last, but never least, I thank Barbara Arvin, who designed the covers for both the first and second editions of this text.

Alice Robertson
Professor of English
Director or Writing
Western Illinois University

Writing Worlds: from Private Places to Public Spaces

Introduction

For the past eight years the Western Illinois University Writing Program has struggled to find a rhetoric that fits into our "from-personal-to-public" writing philosophy and the sequenced assignments that implement that philosophy. We were looking for a rhetoric based on what we believe about the teaching of writing and the ways students develop the analytical language skills they need to become effective consumers (readers) and producers (writers) of texts. Within that overarching goal, we believe in and base our program's agenda on a series of specific pedagogies about the teaching of writing. Simply put, we believe that

- All writing is personal writing because a person produces that writing.
- This beginning, often highly personal, writing is the gateway to public writing in both the academic and "real world" spheres.
- That gateway works since students who are personally invested in their writing tasks write better papers because they care about their topics.
- Creating a series of sequenced assignments, a series of papers that respectively builds on the skills and techniques mastered in previous assignments, is the key to developing students' individual writing abilities over a semester-long course.
- All good writing is rewriting. (Re) vision, (re)seeing the topic and reworking the content, structure and style according to that new vision, is essential for the student writers' development.
- The most effective (re)vision occurs when writers have constructive feedback from both peers and teachers. Therefore, peer and teacher responses are an essential part of every writing assignment.
- As part of this essential response process, students will not be asked to turn in assignments for grading until they have received and had time to review the final responses from their previous papers. Writers cannot improve until they know their own strengths and weaknesses from an audience viewpoint.
- The most important thing we do as writing teachers is to make students aware of their own individual writing processes because, once aware of those processes, they can consciously control them and effectively produce future papers regardless of the particular writing task those papers might involve.

- In order to create this awareness, we encourage a series of self-reflective "process pieces" that accompany every formal assignment and culminate in a final paper, "case study of myself as a writer," the ultimate overarching assignment of our freshman writing course. This meta-cognitive piece focuses on students' strengths and weaknesses, the techniques and skills they have mastered during the semester, and the writing problems they still need to work on in the future. The self awareness essential for a successful case study provides students with the self knowledge they need to succeed in future writing tasks within and beyond the academy.

- Perhaps most important, pedagogically speaking, is our conviction that no one ever successfully taught writing by talking about writing to a class. Students learn to write by writing, every day.

- Therefore, our classrooms are student centered; our teachers employ interactive learning methods and collaborative work to create writing communities that demonstrate how the social construction of knowledge works on a daily basis. Our practices include individual freewriting, in-class group projects, and whole class discussion of assigned material.

Our English 180 course is specifically designed to implement these beliefs to help our students become better writers. How far each student comes in a given semester depends upon where he/she starts. Our students come from all kinds of diverse economic backgrounds, ethnic heritages, and levels of academic preparation. All our writing assignments and all the exercises and homework within each assignment are designed to meet the needs of this widely varied student population. We are fortunate to have relatively small classes (22 per section) taught by either fulltime, experienced instructors or thoroughly trained and supervised teaching assistants. While individual teachers vary their specific class assignments and the activities leading up to those assignments, all focus on the same goals for their students and endorse the same beliefs about the teaching of writing. That agreement is what makes our writing program coherent, cohesive, and effective.

What we as a program lacked until now was a text that specifically supported and developed our particular curriculum. In the past either our textbook choices failed to cover every assignment we wanted, or they covered them in a very different sequence or with a very different emphasis. And always there was a great deal of extraneous material we never used but that added to the cost of the text for our already financially stretched students. Since we were unable to discover an existing text that covered what we wanted, we decided to produce that text ourselves. This text is designed to serve Western Illinois University students because it will be specifically tailored to our English 180 teaching philosophy and writing assignments. Consider this text a working draft, not a final product. In fact, we would greatly appreciate the feedback of both teachers and students using this text this coming year. Tell us what is working and what is not, and we will practice what we preach and rework our material to reflect your feedback to us.

What Is English 180? Who Takes This Course? What Do They Learn?

Before freshman students enter WIU, they are required to write an essay placement exam. The score on this exam determines whether a student is placed in English 100, a developmental course, or in English 180, the first in a two part, freshman–sophomore sequence. In 180, instructors challenge students to write increasingly complex essays that move them away from writing for a high school audience and toward writing for the academy.

Since all sections are taught on rotation (usually every other day) in one of the two computer writing labs in Simpkins on campus, English 180 also introduces students to Western's computer network. Using a simple list serve, or Blackboard, or WebCT, or Western OnLine, students may keep an electronic journal where they respond to class readings, reflect on assignments and peer reviews, and create their own writing community. Moreover, many instructors use the time in the lab to teach internet research skills as they apply to the research paper. In addition to the electronic sources, instructors also take students to the library for instruction in traditional research practices.

This course serves as a bridge between the quick five-paragraph high school essay, written the night before the assignment is due, and the type of well-developed writing expected at the university level.

In fact, it is in English 180 where students are asked, perhaps for the first time, to view writing as a process—one that requires them to make choices based upon a rhetorical situation. Since these initial choices force further decisions, they begin to see how writing for the university can be quite complicated. That's why those who teach English 180 typically break down the writing process in such a way that each paper grows holistically from inception to completion. Initially, an invention technique, such as mapping or listing, leads to a topic. Then, as students develop their topics to fit the parameters of the assignment, teachers act as guides, modeling ways in which the topics might be developed.

In addition, techniques or strategies that are taught for beginning papers can be used again, and built upon, in later papers. This is called sequencing. Skills such as narrative, practiced in a beginning essay that focuses entirely on a student's life experience, can be used in limited form in such genres as the evaluation, the problem/solution paper, or even a researched argument paper. In truth, moving students from writing solely about a personal experience, which is a rather tight focus on the "I," to a place where they can view their experience in the context of a larger worldwide one is part of nudging them to see globally and write academically.

Moreover, although English 180 teachers continually stress the importance of audience awareness, the true test comes when students share their work with classmates during the peer draft class period. In small group work, student essays are read and critiqued by their peers, just as each student reads and critiques the others' essays. At that time, students are truly aware of audience and can begin to see their essays objectively.

Then, working with feedback that their peers, and sometimes their teachers, have provided, each student has the responsibility to revise his or her draft so that it more clearly conforms to the parameters of the individual assignment.

At the end of this part of the process is another key element of English 180: reflection. After each major essay, some teachers have their students write a reflection. The prompts, or questions, focus the students' attention on the rhetorical choices that they have made in order to complete that particular essay. At the end of the semester, other teachers have their students write a complete essay that analyzes their growth as writers over the course of that semester. Indeed, a few teachers do both. These types of reflection reinforce what students have learned and help students begin the process of generalization, as they start to understand that what is taught at the university in one class is applicable in others.

All of these elements, and more, go into the English 180 course.

Course Goals and Objectives

English 180 is the first in a series of required writing courses in the educational program at Western Illinois University. Writing is fundamental in academic life. In the process of writing, a person can discover and clarify information, ideas, judgments, different ways of understanding, and even at times passions and convictions that matter most to him or her. In writing, a person also effectively communicates the information, ideas, judgments, ways of understanding, or convictions to others.

The effective communication of thought is the hallmark of a university education, and in one way or another, it is the goal of most courses in the curriculum. English 180 is intended to help students develop strategies for effective writing and clear thinking so that they may more readily achieve the goals of their own course of study at the university.

In learning to write effectively, students in English 180 will

- make writing choices within the rhetorical context of academic writing with attention to the particular audience, subject matter, and purpose of writing;
- carefully read short texts that include discourse on significant human and intellectual issues;
- use strategies for discovering and connecting insights from reading and their experiences by using, for example:
  - small and large group discussions,
  - invention techniques (questions, cubing, and so on),
  - note-taking,
  - summary,
  - library research;
- write to respond to the concepts and arguments provided in the texts they read, for example:
  - description,
  - explanation,
  - summary;
- give adequate time and attention to each stage in the writing process, that is:
  - inventing,
  - drafting,
  - discussing drafts with others for a sense of audience and clarity,
  - revising and redrafting for coherence and completeness,
  - editing for correctness of expression and presentation,
  - reflecting on the methods by which they have developed their thinking;
- write essays that apply the knowledge gained from reading these texts to their own experiences and that test such knowledge against their own perceptions, for example:
  - comparison,
  - analysis,
  - evaluation;
- organize their ideas effectively by developing a working knowledge of the logical structure underlying English syntax at the sentence level and beyond;
- develop methods for editing their own writing to conform to the accepted standards for print publication (spelling, punctuation, word usage, etc.);
- use computer word processing for drafting, revising, and editing their writing.

Paper Assignments for English 180

This course is based on the concept of using personal writing as a way into academic writing. Assignments are designed to help students utilize their own knowledge and experiences in order to enter and participate in the academic discourse community. Within a personal response format, English 180 assignments attempt to preserve student voices and take advantage of students' interests to generate student writing based on personal involvement topics that lead to academic writing.

Paper #1

A narrative and/or descriptive response to a personal experience.

Paper #2

A revision of paper #1 with an added analysis or self-reflection of the personal experience of Paper #1.

Paper #3

An informal opinion paper based on the student's experiences and beliefs about a significant issue or a descriptive statement explaining a problem the student wishes to deal with for Paper #4.

Paper #4

A short research project on the same topic as Paper #3: It includes a library visit, collaborative group work with sources and research processes, and focus on integrating research material and documentation into the students' texts. The paper itself is a true rewrite (a *re*-visioning of the personal response paper that requires students to rethink, reorganize, and add new material to their original texts) that further develops the skills of summary and analysis of texts and introduces the student to the concept of synthesis on a limited scale.

Paper #5

A timed in-class piece of writing that prepares students to take essay exams in other classes. This involves homework and class work with two or three readings on a topic, the practice formulation of possible essay questions, and the development of thesis statements from those questions; it also includes a series of strategies for studying for and actually taking the essay test. This work further highlights summarizing and synthesizing materials into a coherent piece of writing and teaches students the importance of including references to specific texts in their own papers.

Paper #6

A case study of the student as a writer: This paper cements the student's awareness of his or her own writing processes and is based on materials from the student's writing portfolio from the entire semester: journal entries, teacher and peer feedback, and process sheets for each paper. It is a self-reflective piece that can be written as a narrative tracing the student's progress as a writer for the semester or an essay organized around a particular writing problem or problems.

Follow these assignments specifically. Instructors can alter or substitute other specific assignments, making certain that these substitutes meets the goals of 180.

Readings incorporated into 180 writing assignments:

Paper #1—Minimum of two professional life writing pieces to be read, analyzed, and discussed; these serve as examples of the kinds of topics and organizational strategies students can use to fulfill this assignment. These readings introduce them to analysis of and response to texts in their very first assignment.

Paper #2—At least one longer, more complex autobiographical piece to be read and analyzed and discussed in class with a focus on providing analysis of their own experience in the conclusions of their papers; teachers can also use this additional reading to focus on writing good introductions and adding significant details to personal narratives.

Paper #3—Two long argumentative pieces that each provide pro and con sides of a single issue, or four shorter pieces, covering different issues but with one pro and one con article on each issue. These are to be used in class debates to teach students how to organize arguments, how to provide proof for points made, and how to incorporate the other side into their own persuasive writing.

Paper #4—Read three more persuasive essays (all on one issue), summarize and analyze each, and then synthesize points and ideas to develop a thesis for an argumentative paper, and then work out an organizational chart for a mock position paper documented with these three sources. This serves as a modeling for the process they will use to write their own short research position paper that is developed and expanded from their informal argument.

Paper #5—Assign three or more articles or texts (visuals, audio, etc.) on the same topic; have the class read, analyze, and discuss each, and then identify and synthesize points from all three. The class will then develop possible essay exam questions from this synthesis and then take an in-class essay exam based on those questions.

Paper #6—Reread all the papers, responses from teacher and peers and their own process sheets to review and reflect upon their own writing processes and progress during the semester.

Part One
Course Overview

A. What to Expect in the First Two Weeks

Because we believe that all writing is personal and that student investment in individual papers is essential for successful writing, we begin our course with a comparison of two seemingly distinctively different kinds of writing: private and public. For you, the student, private writing is just what the name implies, *private*, produced <u>by</u> you *for* you and no one else. In other words, you are your own audience for private writing. In this situation, you don't need to spell out everything precisely or define every term or abbreviation you use because <u>you</u> know what <u>you</u> are trying to say. Often a private shorthand works quite well if you are your only reader. Conversely, public writing is loosely defined as any writing you produce for a reader or readers other than yourself. Such writing can be as formal as a scholarly essay for a college class or as informal as a letter home to your parents. If someone else is intended to read what you are writing, then that piece is public writing because it has an external audience.

Both kinds of writing are governed by what writing teachers label "the rhetorical situation," an occasion determined by a series of simple questions:

- Who is writing what?
- To whom are they writing?
- Why are they writing?

The first question concerns the "what" or subject of the writing (S) and the "who" or writer of the piece (W). Question two concerns the audience to whom the piece is addressed (A); and question three, the "Why," is, of course, the purpose of the piece, the reason you are writing it in the first place or what you hope to accomplish by writing it (P). Simply put, the rhetorical situation for any writing task can be determined by identifying these four factors:

S—Subject or topic of the writing task
W—Writer fulfilling the task
A—Audience addressed by that writer
P—Purpose or reason for the writing task

Because you, like every other writer, must answer those questions to position yourself within a given rhetorical situation, we use these four factors to design our first week of English 180 to familiarize you with the differences between private and public writing.

We take you through a series of hands-on, in-class writing tasks covering both kinds of writing and then let you discover these differences for yourself through discussion with your fellow classmates.

Next, in week two, we focus on particular rhetorical situations, especially their audiences and purposes. Here we start to make you aware of the general or generic writing processes we will use in producing each one of the six assignments in the course.

1. the pre-writing steps of invention and discovery, as well as those of evaluating, selecting and then organizing material;
2. the actual writing phase; and
3. the post-writing stages of response, rewriting, editing, and proofreading.

No one sits down and composes *Hamlet* or *Lord of the Rings* or even a pop music review for a high school newspaper at one sitting. Good writing always includes generating relevant materials from your own knowledge or informal or formal research, creating a draft, receiving feedback from readers, and redrafting with the needs of those readers (your audience) in mind. These are the generic processes all writers go through, and we as writing teachers take you through them step by step.

But there are also specific writing processes for each individual writer, processes that vary a great deal from writer to writer. What you do when you write a paper is not necessarily what your classmates do when they write papers. You may, for example, listen to certain CDs while you compose on a computer late at night. The student sitting beside you in class may prefer to sit outside under a tree and write with a pen on a legal pad. A third needs absolute quiet in the library and needs to chew gum while drafting a paper. The point is that there are as many different individual writing processes as there are students in a writing class. Therefore, we cannot teach these processes because they are idiosyncratic, or specific to each individual student. All we can do as writing teachers is to make you as a writer aware of your own processes because, once you are conscious of these processes, you can control them and produce a paper for any assigned writing task. That is the real goal of 180, to make you an effective, competent writer. The six assignments in this book are designed and sequenced to do just that, to take you from brief, informal freewrites through informal and formal writing situations that lead you to produce both formal academic papers and real world writing assignments in the end. The skills you acquire writing each paper are necessary for the next assignment; each subsequent paper is longer and more complex, but each builds on what you learned fulfilling the previous assignments. All the papers are based on particular topics you choose from within a general subject framework provided by your teacher. English 180 is not difficult if you keep up, going step by step through the curriculum requirements. This book is designed as a kind of guide or road map for that process.

*****

B. Personal Writing, Public Writing

All writing is personal writing because, regardless of the situation or assignment, a <u>person</u> is always doing the writing. The premise of this writing course is moving student writers from private, informal personal writing intended for an internal audience only to public, formal personal writing in a recognizable genre intended for an external audience. Recognizing the different requirements of each of these kinds of writing enables student writers to move from one to the other more easily. Two simple writing exercises the first week of class followed by group analysis and whole-class discussion make those differences apparent.

Whether private or public, a grocery list or an editorial, all writing tasks have a purpose, a reason for the writing to take place. You can personally write to create (a story, a poem, an explanation, etc.) or to discover (uncovering relationships, connections, or patterns within ideas),but most public writing focuses on communication, transmitting ideas or information to an external audience. In academic writing the purpose of these public writing tasks varies with individual assignments. You may be asked to

- explain an idea, a situation, an event, or a process to an audience that knows less than you do about the topic,
- argue a position and persuade your audience to agree with you
- or analyze a text, situation, or event to determine what it means and then convey that meaning to your audience

Or your assignment may combine more than one of these purposes.

To accomplish any purpose, writers must focus on their audience, the readers addressed in the writing task. And the more writers know about a specific audience, the better their chances of reaching that audience and accomplishing that purpose. Unless specifically otherwise assigned by an instructor, our college assignments simultaneously address three separate but equally important audiences in this specific order:

1. the writers themselves
2. their peers (fellow classmates who will respond to an early draft)
3. their instructor who will respond and ultimately grade the paper itself

---

Exercise for Private Writing/Public Discourse

This in-class exercise is designed to make you aware of the similarities and differences between private writing and public discourse.

Step One—Private Free Writing:

Take out a blank sheet of paper and a pen (or use the computer keyboard if you are in a computer classroom) and free write about anything you wish for ten minutes. Do not worry about spelling or grammar or punctuation or paragraphing; no one but you will ever see this writing. You are writing to yourself only. The only requirements are that you put the pen on the paper and do not stop writing for the allotted time. Do not stop to scratch through something or go back to make corrections. Just write nonstop about whatever comes into your mind for ten minutes.

Step Two—Public Discourse:

Now take out another sheet of paper (or return to the keyboard) and write a letter to me, the teacher, about your expectations for this course. What do you want to learn in this class? What in your writing needs to be improved? What are your goals for this course? Remember, I will take up this assignment and read it and respond to it and return it next period.

Now, form groups of four or five people to discuss the two kinds of writing you have just done in this class. Each group is responsible for completing the following tasks in writing:

- Make a list of the similarities and a list of the differences in the two kinds of writing.
- Discuss those lists and try to reach consensus as a group about which one you prefer.
- Make a list of the reasons for your choice to share with the class.
- Report your group work to the class as a whole for discussion.

SWAP Exercise

Note: As you may need to view this a couple of times, this activity works better if the TV commercial has been taped and can be replayed.

Watch a TV commercial, closely, and answer the following questions:

1. **Subject:** Determine the message, the speaker's main idea of what he/she/it wants to convince you to agree with, understand, or purchase.
2. **Writer:** Analyze the speaker. Using only the advertisement as a source of evidence, respond to the following:
   a. Facts about the speaker (company or ad-creator)
   b. The speaker's attitude toward the product
3. **Audience:** Determine the audience. Who is the ad targeting? What details are included that bring you to your conclusion?
4. **Purpose:** Determine the purpose, the change the speaker is trying to bring about in the audience's knowledge, action, or way of thinking about something.

In other words, first get your thoughts down on paper in a rough draft, clarify and then organize them into whatever format the assignment requires. In this stage you are writing to yourself for yourself. Second, submit that first formatted draft to the peer responding process in class. Third, analyze the peer feedback, accepting or rejecting suggestions that do or do not work toward improving the paper. Fourth, rewrite that first draft incorporating the feedback you felt was most helpful and submit that draft for teaching response and/or grading. In most papers, especially the longer, more difficult assignments, individual or group conferences with your instructor will precede grading, and you will have another chance to redraft with a second set of feedback suggestions. For other shorter, less complicated papers, the instructor may provide feedback and a grade simultaneously, offering the opportunity to revise to anyone who did poorly on the second draft. In that case, doing the second optional rewrite is up to each individual student.

As we explained before the SWAP exercise, each assignment will include the three generic stages of the writing process. Based on the stages of classical rhetoric, these processes are

Prewriting
Writing
Rewriting

Let us examine each briefly before we begin to use them in Paper #1.

Prewriting

Part of invention in classical rhetoric, prewriting includes all activities a writer undertakes to decide on a topic and then generate, locate, or discover ideas to include in writing about that topic. In the prewriting stage in this course for every assignment we include

- prewriting exercises like freewriting, listing, clustering, etc., to help you focus and select a topic and then generate information about that topic
- a list of appropriate readings in the same genre as the assignment to give you the opportunity to become familiar with that genre and the ways other writers have chosen to develop it

- at least one student paper as an example of how Western students fulfill that assignment
- when appropriate, questions to help you determine and analyze your audience

Writing

For the actual writing we incorporate out-of-class time and in-class workshopping to allow you to work on your own while still getting help from your instructor and your peers. In-class writing time often focuses on specific aspects of the paper—for example, working on introductions, conclusions, transitions, or development of detail or evidence. Drafting is getting your ideas down in some relevant order; you cannot improve and polish your writing until you have something written down to work with.

Rewriting

All good writing includes rewriting, or revision; and revision is (re)vision or re-seeing the topic and the organization all over again. It can mean deleting material, adding material, and/or reorganizing material by moving individual sentences or whole paragraphs within the text. Re(vision) can be seeing the topic from an entirely different angle or perspective. For example, in argument, it can even be reversing your position on a given topic and arguing against your original position. Revision can even mean scrapping your first draft and starting over, if that's what needs to be done to successfully accomplish the assignment. Your rewriting includes reworking the rough draft with peer feedback and the resulting second draft with instructor feedback (with or without a grade). Details of these three processes are specifically worked out in each subsequent chapter with each of the six paper assignments in this class.

C. The Importance of Critical Reading in the Writing Class

Reading and writing are two sides of the same language coin, and both are dependent on each other. Both processes use language, words arranged in certain orders, to convey meaning, to communicate with ourselves and others. The difference between writing and reading is obvious. Writing is the *production* of a text using language you as writer create to encode meaning for yourself and/or others to decipher. You write to communicate meaning for yourself and for others. A writer is, after all, always someone with something to say. Conversely, reading is the *consumption* of a text created by using language. In reading, you, or the audience (the reader), decipher the meaning originally encoded by either yourself or someone else.

Both processes require a knowledge of the way language works and of the grammar, vocabulary, and mechanics of a given language. But they also involve the way all these work together to help you, as a writer or a reader, to communicate or discover meaning in a particular text. Years of research tell us that the best writers are also the best readers. The more you read and absorb the complexities of language, the better and more effectively you manipulate that language when you write. You know that reading is more than scanning all the words on a page. How many times have you read every word of a chapter in a text as homework and not known what you read when you finished? Critical reading is reading for meaning, carefully analyzing what you read, being aware of, not only *what* is being said, but *how* it is being said as well. To succeed in today's world, people need to be able to understand the texts—written, oral, and visual—that bombard them daily. Thus, no writing class would be complete without a reading component to develop your analytical and critical language skills. The more you sharpen those skills, the more success you will have, in college and in your chosen profession. The more you read, the better writer you will become.

If critical reading is reading for meaning, reading to understand *what* is being said and *how* that meaning is being conveyed, then learning to read critically rather than just reading words on a page is a skill you must cultivate and practice to succeed in the academy and the rest of the world. The best way to begin that process is to employ six basic steps in all your serious reading:

1. Highlight or underline what you feel are the key words and sentences of the text.
2. Bracket important passages with a colored marker.
3. Connect related ideas with lines (in the text) by inserting your own marginal comments.
4. Circle words to be defined and look them up.
5. Outline main ideas in the margin in your own words.
6. Write brief comments and questions for discussion in the margin.

Using those six steps, complete the following critical reading activity in groups as class work.

Critical Reading Activity

1. Go to www.lyrics.com and pick out a favorite song.
2. Often, although we "know" the words to our favorite songs and can sing along, we never really consider what these songs are about.
3. Following the six steps above, critically read the lyrics to the song you've chosen.
4. Now, what is this song actually about? Is there a story or a statement within these lyrics? Share your interpretation with your classmates.

Briefly, we have just defined and outlined English 180 for you. Now, let's get specific and start writing.

Part Two
The Personal Narrative

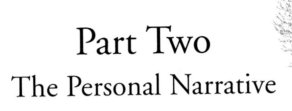

ASSIGNMENT ONE: The Personal Narrative

"Write what you know," creative writing teachers tell their students. Composition teachers often translate that advice into, "Write about something you care about, something that matters to you." They say that because only then will you be invested in your writing, and only when you are invested in your writing will you produce good, effective papers. If you combine both pieces of advice, write what you know and care about, you fulfill our assignment #1, the personal narrative. Here you choose a specific, single event in your life (or in a variation, pick a particular person who influenced you) and describe it in detail for your teacher and fellow classmates. You are, quite simply, telling a story about yourself or someone else who has played an important part in shaping your life.

To prepare you for this assignment, we will write collaborative narratives together to master the tricks of the narrative trade: structure, coherence, and clarity. To see how other writers describe similar events in their lives, we will read several personal narratives and talk about them together as a class to discover ways to better tell our own stories. To help you write your own personal narrative, we will devote class time to developing introductions, working on the main "body" of each story, and writing effective conclusions.

*****

Definition of Assignment: Your personal narrative tells a personal story about you. It is based on an event in your life, one you choose because of its significance to you; it is something that matters a great deal to you; it is so important that you choose to write about it and share it with your peers and your instructor. And you want to tell it in such a way as to make them—your readers—see that event through your eyes. A great author, Joseph Conrad, once said:

> *My job as a writer is to make you see, to make you hear, to make you feel, but it is above all, to make you see.*

That's what great writers do, what all good writers try to do—to make you, the reader, see the story through the writer's eyes. And that's what you as a writer want to try to do—to get us, your readers, to see your story through your eyes. To do that, you need to

- First, choose an event that was truly significant, that made a difference in the rest of your life.
- Second, make the sequence of the story, the action, as clear and complete as possible.
- Third, develop that event with as much detail as possible—the scene, the people, the action, etc.

To help you accomplish this assignment, we provide a series of prewriting exercises.

Prewriting

#1—The Time Line

> - Draw a horizontal line all the way across a blank sheet of paper.
> - The beginning of the line is the year you were born; the end of the line is today.
>
> ```
> ***************************************************************
>      Birth                                    Today
>   X_____X
>      4/1980                                   8/2009
> ***************************************************************
> ```
>
> - Now plot every important event you remember in your life from your birth to the present with an x on the time line. Date each x by year and month if possible and identify it by a labeling work or phrase. Some events may be public—first grade starts—others private—the death of a pet or family member. What matters is that all the events matter to you.
> - Now select one experience on your time line to write about. Name it and give the reason for your choice by writing and completing this sentence:
>
>   "I am going to tell you about a time when _____
>
>   because _____."

Just in case you are stuck and can't decide what to choose from your time line, here is a list general topics other students have used for successful papers in the past. Perhaps one of them may fit an event on your time line; if it does not, feel free to adapt it for your own personal experience narrative.

- The first time you were really afraid
- The death of a family member
- The change in a relationship
- Your first job
- The loss of a friend
- Leaving home for the first time
- A risk-taking experience
- Learning how to do something for the first time
- Body images

Finishing this exercise begins your personal narrative paper. You have your topic and your rationale for choosing it. You have your point of view—a personal approach using the informal "I." You have your audience—the class. Now you are ready to begin your story by Freewriting

Freewriting is a great way to begin each class because it is a kind of warming-up exercise for writers. Think in terms of piano playing. Students often "warm up" with a set of exercises before they play a complete piece. Or think of an athletic team "warming up" before the actual game—flexing the right muscles and getting into the mindset to play. Freewriting allows writers to do the same thing—to flex and exercise the writing muscle before using it in a full-blown writing task. But freewriting is for more than just warm-up practice. It can be used to discover ideas, to try out topics, and even to develop details about topics already chosen—describing a character or a scene in a story, for example. And it's a no-risk way of trying out ideas you may find useful later.

Here is a series of informal freewrites that offer practice writing in narrative situations:

> - Pick a scar somewhere on your body. Tell the story of how that happened.
> - What was the moment when you realized you weren't a kid anymore?
> - If you had to pick the most important moment in your entire life, what would it be?
> - What's the most important lesson you ever learned?
> - If you could give one piece of advice to incoming freshmen, what would it be and why?
> - If you could change one thing that happened in your life, what would it be and why did you choose it?

#2—Generating Material

To generate material for your narrative, ask yourself a series of questions about the event you have chosen:

1. When did the event occur? How old were you?
2. Where did it occur?
3. Under what conditions did it occur? Think of weather, surroundings, your own physical, mental, and/or emotional state (Were you hurt? Upset?)
4. Who was involved in the event? List the people and identify them in relation to you and the event—for example, "my best friend who was driving the car when we crashed."
5. What background do I need to give my readers about me, the event, the others involved, etc., in order for those readers to understand my story?
6. Do I need physical descriptions of the people, the place, etc.?
7. Do I need dialogue? If so, who should speak and at what point in the story?

> A good brief class exercise is to see if anyone can add to this list of questions. Answering these questions should generate more than enough material to flesh out your story.

In-class collaborative exercises always help students to master the process of completing a particular assignment because they can repeat the collaborative process when they write their individual papers. The in-class group work is a kind of dry run for the actual writing assignment.

#3—In-Class Collaborative Narratives

Collaborative practice of personal experience (four people to a group)

> Give members of each group a choice of topic:
>   1. a tough situation when you had to make a difficult choice
>   2. an incident that did not turn out the way you thought it would
>   3. an encounter with another person that changed your life
>   4. a person who surprised or disappointed you
>   5. someone you admire, envy, disapprove of, or are fascinated with
>
> Now every person in the group writes an introductory paragraph, introducing the "me" of the story and the setting (time and place). 4 minutes
> Each person passes his or her paper to the right.
> Now each person writes paragraph two: the other people involved in the story and the details of the circumstances—except of course each is writing the second paragraph to someone else's introductory paragraph, so they must first read it and tailor their paragraph to fit that introduction. 5 minutes
> Pass each paper to the right again.
> Now each person writes paragraph 3—the event, incident, or problem, what happens that has to be resolved—but first each has to read the two preceding paragraphs and make their third paragraph fit. 6 minutes
> Pass each paper to the right again.
> Now each person reads the first three paragraphs and writes paragraph four, the resolution. 7 minutes
> Now pass each paper to the right one more time. Each person should have his or her original paper back. Read through the other paragraphs and write a conclusion.
> Share the narratives by letting each student read his/hers to the group. Each group selects one to read aloud to the class.

This collaborative exercise has been group practice writing assignment #1. By participating you have learned the requirements of the genre and

- to introduce the scene and the characters of a story,
- to transition or link the paragraphs of the narrative together,
- to follow the chronological structure of narrative action—introduce the event, create the problem, develop a climax, and a resolution,
- to include detail in your writing to better reach your reader.

Reading

Only one thing remains to do in your prewriting activities: Reading. To better produce your own personal experience narrative, you should examine one or two successful ones from professional writers to see how they handle this kind of writing task. You can identify and analyze the elements of narrative—point of view, characterization, dialogue, description, action—and see how to better incorporate them into your own personal experience writing. And you should read at least one good example of student writing in this genre just to see just how good beginning writers can be in this genre.

Possible narrative examples for readings (including texts from other than print media) are

Print:

"How I Learned the Power of Writing," Richard Bullock
"All Over But the Shouting," Rick Bragg
"Literacy Behind Bars," Malcolm X
"A Shirt Full of Beer," Bill McKibben
"Us and Them," David Sedaris
"Seoul Searching," Rick Reilly
"Grounded for Life," _____

Television:

Any single episode of *Scrubs* or *M*A*S*H*, or any other series with straightforward narration. Half-hour programs work best because the class can view one in 22 minutes and then spend the remaining class time responding to and analyzing the narrative.

Classes should choose at least one example to examine together before writing the first draft of Assignment #1. Individual print narratives can be downloaded and read as homework, with students using the six steps of critical reading and then discussed in class using a series of instructor- and/or student-generated questions like

1. Who are the characters involved? List them and explain their relation to each other.
2. Where and when does the story take place? Describe this setting.
3. What is the chief event or crisis the characters must deal with?
4. How is the crisis resolved?
5. What struck you most about the story? Why?
6. What did you notice that can help you in writing your story?

*****

After examining professional narratives to see how they work and what techniques they use that you may want to adapt, you should also read examples of real students' personal narratives, stories Western students wrote about themselves to fulfill this assignment. Knowing how others like you have dealt with this writing task can help you in writing your own narrative.

Making the Cut
By Jackson Courter

High on the walls of the gym at Edison Elementary School, heavy ventilations fans labored to bring fresh air into the brown, gloomy, industrial-looking space. My team-mates and I ran lazily through simple passing and shooting drills as a young coach's assistant named Rob looked on, half-supervising us. This scene could have been taken from any weeknight basketball practice in the last thirty days, but on this particular night, my attention, and everyone else's attention, was fixed on the door to the locker room. After my part of a drill was done for the moment (and sometimes while in the midst of a drill), I would glance at the door, wondering what was being said on the other side, wondering how much longer till I would be on the other side, wondering what would be said then.

Tonight was cut night. The preseason roster of the eighth-grade Macomb Junior High basketball team would have to drop two or three players for the regular season, and I was on the bubble, not sure if the coaches would keep me or cut me, not even sure if I wanted to remain on the team, since I wouldn't get much playing time if I did. I hadn't played organized basketball since sixth grade (and that was in a small, relatively-relaxed Catholic-school program) but had recently rediscovered my latent passion for the game. So, with the encouragement of Steve, my best friend and team-mate, I decided to try out for the eighth-grade team. But perhaps I wanted to enjoy the school year without having to discipline myself for countless basketball practices and games I wouldn't play in. Perhaps I would decide not to play on the team that season and, instead, practice on my own, hoping to return my freshman year with a sharpened skill set. Or maybe I would just get cut.

As I began to become absorbed in my thoughts and forget that the moment of truth was imminent, a teammate (who had made the team) told me to go see the coach. So, repressing the trembling in my limbs, I headed to the locker room. Face to face with Coach Clauson, a half-tough, half-kindhearted middle-aged man, I tried not to smile too profoundly when he told me "You are one of the guys we're going to keep." Then he said I wouldn't see much playing time but encouraged me to keep training hard. He didn't reiterate the offer he made a few nights earlier to bubble play-ers, that we could voluntarily withdraw from the team if we didn't want to stay, but I knew it still applied—I had only to turn in my preseason jersey at the end of practice and go home, never to endure anymore grueling sprints, drills, or pushups for the rest of the year.

For a moment I couldn't make up my mind. I walked back onto the court, repeat-edly running through all the pros and cons of both sides of the decision. Then I looked at the team, remembering that these guys were my friends—I didn't want to walk out on them, and most importantly, they didn't want to see me go. Steve—who was a bubble player himself, had made the team, and was staying—glanced at me, silently asking me if I had made it, if I was on board for the long haul. I grinned, gave a thumbs up, and said in our corny basketball lingo, "Guess I'm ballin' with this crew."

After practice, as I walked through the biting breeze of mid-November to my dad waiting in our van, I realized that no uncertainty ever truly existed about whether I would stay on the team or not. Even though I truly had to choose to stay, that choice was inevitable—I had been committed ever since I decided to try out for the team in the first place. I couldn't nullify my struggle to make the cut by just walking away.

I got in the van, and my dad asked the same silent question Steve had asked, and I said, "I'm on the team."

The Part
Kendra Moore
Paper #1

It was my junior year in high school when I realized one of my true passions. This passion is the art of theatre. At my small school, we held one play a year. I had been in some of the plays before this, but I had never had a leading role. This year I had tried out for a part in the play, <u>Cheaper By the Dozen</u>. Being in a school that only had forty-eight students made it difficult to put on plays (especially plays that require at least fifteen people) but I knew I had a chance of getting a part. I did my audition in front of the drama club sponsor, but the rest was up to him. Later that day he found me in the hallway; to my excitement; I had received the part of the eldest daughter, Anne.

Rehearsals, memorizing lines, costume fittings, and much more were pieces to creating this play. The cast was assembled, and it consisted of fifteen people. Most of them were high school students but there were few that were from the grade school. Each of us were handed a script to memorize and "become" the character. It was difficult to memorize approximately three hundred lines, this was a task to undertake. I studied lines with other cast members and I read the play over several times to complete this task. Soon it was time to rehearse on stage. This was an interesting feat. Many had never acted before, so you can imagine how long the rehearsals lasted. Due to this circumstance, all of us had to learn the stage directions and where the microphones were. The first few rehearsals were very interesting. Having a wide variety of age groups present, we had to repeat stage directions and where to place your body (which way you were facing) before we could move on to the next act. Even though this was necessary to go through, it was an inconvenience to keep repeating. After everyone knew the stage directions and where the microphones were, we started rehearsing our lines and movements. This was my favorite part. This was where we all got to test how we wanted to make our characters appear to the audience. We had the chance to make our characters come alive and believable. During these rehearsals, I believed that I found how to portray my character. I felt like I was the eldest of the twelve Gilberth children. I was the child that was the "rebel" of the family, wanting my freedom from my father's strict ways. I guess this is what our drama sponsor wanted. He wanted us to become our characters, and I think that was accomplished by most of us. At the costume fittings, I had a great time. I tried on several different outfits to see which three were the best for my character. During making this decision, a couple of us decided we were going to try on various other options that were available at the costume shop. After a couple of hours of trying on clothes and other costumes; we made our decisions. Wearing these outfits on stage made the whole play come together.

After all the rehearsing, memorizing, fittings, lighting, sets, and minor complications, it was the night of the performance. The house was packed, the nerves were up, and everything was ready to go. Behind the curtain, everyone was looking over their lines before they went on stage. The crew was making sure all the right props were in their correct spaces, the lights pointing in the right spot, and that all of the actors were on the same page. During the performance, there were only a few mistakes. These mistakes were not noticeable to the audience, which was good. Overall, the performance went over well. The audience laughed, sighed, and were silent at all the right places. For once in my life, I felt like I was free to express my feelings and that I actually belonged somewhere in the world. I was a part of making this audience feel joy and entertainment for that evening.

continues

The Part (*Continued*)
Kendra Moore
Paper #1

This performance was one of the best times of my life. The nerves before going on stage, wondering if I would mess up on lines or cues, or trip made the whole experience worth it to me. That is when I realized this was what I really loved. The stage was where I could "become" someone else and not worry what others thought. Because on stage, you separate yourself from the character. This way no one could rightfully judge you. You are only playing a part. Being a part of the <u>Cheaper By the Dozen</u> play brought this to my attention. I could let all of my personal emotions out without having to worry about what others thought of me because I knew that all they saw was my character, and they did not know what my true emotions were.

Writing

Now it's time to begin actually drafting that personal narrative you began with the timeline exercise. Whether you use that event or choose another at this point is entirely up to you.

Assignment # 1: Personal Narrative

Write a 2–3 page Personal Narrative (autobiography) paper about a significant event or person in your life.

Using the timeline you developed, choose your event or person carefully with your readers in mind. This paper is public prose that will be shared with your classmates and me; therefore, make your choice with two factors in mind:

1. Your narrative should be one you are comfortable presenting to others.
2. Your narrative should have a general significance that will lead readers to think about the similarities and/or differences between their life experiences and the one you choose to describe.

Possible Topics:

- A time when you made a difficult choice
- A person who changed your mind about something
- An occasion when something did not turn out the way you thought it would
- A person who really surprised or disappointed you
- A person you admire, or despise, envy, or disapprove of
- The most important day in your life
- An event that changed the rest of your life

Hints

- Show, don't tell. For example, rather than writing, "I was so angry," show the anger by writing something like, "my blood churned, rolling over itself in fiery waves and crashing to my fingertips." On a broader spectrum, rather than stating, "I loved my grandpa; he was the kindest man I knew," you have to <u>prove</u> this by showing your grandfather's kindness through a story.
- Hook me; make me want to read this paper from the start (the more interested I am, the easier I grade!).

- Resist the typical, generic events that any of your classmates might write about: the winning football game, summer vacation, your first boyfriend or girlfriend, or graduation day. If you do choose one of these usual topics, develop a unique angle. You need to own this moment that you're writing about and show that it's personal.
- Present your experience/moment dramatically (for example, use dialogue when appropriate, active verbs, vivid adjectives, or flashbacks). Let your readers SEE for themselves what it was like for you to have this experience.
- Carefully choose words and phrases that you feel convey the significance of this narrative to your readers.

Criteria

- <u>Purpose</u>: Does this paper have a clear purpose—to entertain and excite, to evoke sadness or empathy or humor—and does it fulfill that purpose?
- <u>Action</u>: Does the action (events) of the narrative flow well and create an understandable and logical story? If it is unclear what is happening, then the paper is not succeeding in this task.
- <u>Presentation</u>: Have you presented your narrative well? Is there good use of dialogue, description, and conflict? Has the paper been proofread for basic mechanical issues? I do not expect perfect grammar—no one understands all the workings of our language—but it must make sense!

Activities

Workshopping papers in class helps students draft the first version of their papers. But to be effective, workshopping must be specific; it must target one or more particular aspects of the assignment that students find problematical. In personal narratives those aspects almost always include

- Opening (introductions)
- Closing (conclusions)
- Detailed descriptions
- Incorporating dialogue

The following exercises target these particular problems.

Openings and Closings

There are several ways a writer can begin a story.

Some tell the story from a first person perspective and begin with a significant point in the narrator's life:

In my younger and more vulnerable years my father gave me some advice that I've been turning over in my mind ever since.

"Whenever you feel like criticizing anyone," he told me, "just remember that all the people in this world haven't had the advantages that you've had."

He didn't say any more but we've always been unusually communicative in a reserved way and I understood that he meant a great deal more than that. In consequence I'm inclined to reserve all judgments, a habit that has opened up many curious natures to me and also made me the victim of not a few veteran bores.

The Great Gatsby by F. Scott Fitzgerald

Some begin the narrative by incorporating dialogue:

"To the man who loves art for its own sake," remarked Sherlock Holmes, tossing aside the advertisement of The Daily Telegraph, "it is frequently in its least important and lowliest manifestations that the keenest pleasure is to be deprived. It is pleasant to me to observe, Watson, that you have so far grasped this truth that in these little records of our cases which you have been good enough to draw up, and, I am bound to say, occasionally to embellish, you have given prominence not so much to the many causes célèbres and sensational trials in which I have figured but rather to those incidents which may have been trivial in themselves, but which have given room for those faculties of deduction and of logical synthesis which I have made my special province."

"The Adventure of the Copper Beeches" by Sir Arthur Conan Doyle

The use of dialogue should try to be authentic as well, including dialects and slang.

"Father!"
"What is it?"
"What are them men diggin' over there in the field for?"
There was a sudden dropping and enlarging of the lower part of the old man's face, as if some heavy weight had settled therein; he shut his mouth tight, and went on harnessing the great bay mare. He hustled the collar on to her neck with a jerk.
"Father!"
The old many slapped the saddle upon the mare's back.
"Look here, father, I want to know what them men are diggin' over in the field for, an' I'm goin' to know."
"I wish you'd go into the house, mother, an' 'tend to your own affairs," the old man said then. He ran his words together, and his speech was almost as inarticulate as a growl.

"The Revolt of 'Mother'" by Mary E. Wilkins Freeman

Some begin with a detailed description of an important setting:

The studio was filled with the rich odour of roses, and when the light summer wind stirred amidst the trees of the garden, there came through the open door the heavy scent of the lilac, or the more delicate perfume of the pink-flowering thorn.
From the corner of the divan of Persian saddle-bags on which he was lying, smoking, as was his custom, innumerable cigarettes, Lord Henry Wotton could just catch the gleam of the honey-sweet and honey-coloured blossoms of a laburnum, whose tremulous branches seemed hardly able to bear the burden of a beauty so flame-like as theirs; and now and then the fantastic shadows of birds in flight flitted across the long tussore-silk curtains that were stretched in front of the huge window, producing a kind of momentary Japanese effect, and making him think of those pallid jade-faced painters of Tokio, . . .

The Picture of Dorian Gray by Oscar Wilde

Some give the reader insight into what kind of "person" a given character is:

Her doctor had told Julian's mother that she must lost twenty pounds on account of her blood pressure, so on Wednesday nights Julian had to take her downtown on the bus for a reducing class at the Y. The reducing class was designed for working girls over fifty, who weighed from 165 to 200 pounds. His mother was one of the slimmer ones, but she said ladies did not tell their age or weight. She would not ride the buses by herself at night since they had been integrated, and because the reducing class was one of her few pleasures, necessary for her health, and free, she said Julian could at least put himself out to take her, considering all she did for him. Julian did not like to consider all she did for him, but every Wednesday night he braced himself and took her.

"Everything That Rises Must Converge" by Flannery O'Connor

Others give elaborate physical descriptions:

He was a skinny, black-haired, bespectacled boy who had the pinched, slightly unhealthy look of someone who has grown a lot in a short space of time. His jeans were torn and dirty, his T-shirt baggy and faded, and the soles of his trainers were peeling away from the uppers.

<u>Harry Potter and the Order of the Phoenix</u> by J.K. Rowling

These examples are by no means exhaustive of the many ways a narrative can begin. Some narratives even integrate multiple techniques into the introduction. Most commonly, background information and introduction of characters are included in the introduction of the narrative. The writer must decide what is important to bring into the beginning. Some of these questions may help decide in what way you want to begin the narrative:

- Where, in the chronology of the events, do you want to begin? The beginning, middle, or end?
- From what point of view do you want to tell the story? First person introspective? Third person? Is this written as the events happen or written looking back on events that happened in the past?
- Do you want to include dialogue? Describe a character or the setting? Describe events from before the narrative that are important to the narrative itself.

Remember, not every movie starts at the very beginning of the story. You don't either.

Ultimately, the decision of how to start the narrative is yours and what you feel would best grab the interest of the reader, ensuring a captivated audience throughout the story.

- -

Like the introduction, the conclusion can take several different forms.

Some tie up the loose ends, explaining everything that has happened beyond the scope of the narrative:

And thus was solved the mystery of the sinister house with the copper beeches in front of the door. Mr. Rucastle survived, but was always a broken man, kept alive solely through the care of his devoted wife. They still live with their old servants, who probably know so much of Rucastle's past life that he finds it difficult to part from them. Mr. Fowler and Miss Rucastle were married, by special license, in Southampton the day after their flight, and he is now the holder of a government appointment in the island of Mauritius. As to Miss Violet Hunter, my friend Holmes, rather to my disappointment, manifested no further interest in her when once she had ceased to be the centre of one of his problems, and she is now the head of a private school at Walsall, where I believe that she has met with considerable success.

"The Adventure of the Copper Beeches" by Sir Arthur Conan Doyle

Conversely, some leave the ending very open:

> Then they discussed their situation for a long time, trying to think how they could get rid of the necessity for hiding, deception, living in different towns, being so long without meeting. How were they to shake off these intolerable fetters"
>
> "How? How?" he repeated, clutching his head. "How?"
>
> And it seemed to them that they were within an inch of arriving at a decision, and that then a new, beautiful life would begin. And they both realized that the end was still far, far away, and that the hardest, the most complicated part was only just beginning.

"The Lady with the Dog" by Anton Chekov

If the story is told from a first person point of view, consider reflecting on the significance:

> I did not know what had happened to the birds. Perhaps they had gone away to some far place of belonging. Perhaps they had been unable to find such a place, and had simply died out, having ceased to care any longer whether they lived or not.
>
> I remembered how Piquette had scorned to come along, when my father and I sat there and listened to the lake birds. It seemed to me now that in some unconscious and totally unrecognizable way, Piquette might have been the only one, after all, who had heard the crying of the loons.

"The Loons" by Margaret Laurence

Again, think of this as a movie. Think of these questions to help you picture how you see the narrative ending:

Do you want to tie up all the loose ends, or do you want your reader to want more?

Do you want the narrative to simply relate the events as they happen or do you want the narrator (either in first or third person) to think about the significance of whatever happened?

The decisions are limitless. The choice is yours to make this narrative the best it can be.

Sometimes students get stuck. They just can't come up with that first line. To help them, here are some of the greatest first lines in literature. In groups, choose one and write the rest of the opening paragraph. Compare your group's paragraph to the original. Discuss the differences.

Famous First Lines

Marley was dead, to begin with. There is no doubt whatever about that. ("A Christmas Carol," Charles Dickens)

In a·hole in the ground there lived a hobbit. (*The Hobbit,* J. R. R. Tolkein)

Call me Ishmael. (*Moby Dick,* Herman Melville)

It was the best of times, it was the worst of times, it was the age of wisdom, it was the age of foolishness, it was the epoch of belief, it was the epoch of incredulity, it was the season of Light, it was the season of Darkness, it was the spring of hope, it was the winter of despair, we had everything before us, we had nothing before us, we were all going direct to Heaven, we were all going direct the other way—in short, the period was so. (*A Tale of Two Cities,* Charles Dickens)

It was a pleasure to burn. (*Fahrenheit 451,* Ray Bradbury)

This is not for you. (*House of Leaves,* Mark Z. Danielewski)

A Long Time Ago, In a Galaxy Far, Far Away (*Star Wars,* George Lucas)

Mother died today (*The Stranger,* Albert Camus)

It was a dark and stormy night (*A Wrinkle in Time,* Madeline L'Engle)

This is a tale of a meeting of two lonesome, skinny, fairly old white men on a planet which was dying fast. (*Breakfast of Champions,* Kurt Vonnegut)

What's it going to be then, eh? (*A Clockwork Orange,* Anthony Burgess)

All this happened, more or less (*Slaughterhouse Five,* Kurt Vonnegut)

The great fish moved silently through the night water, propelled by short sweeps of its crescent tail. (*Jaws,* Peter Benchley)

It is a truth universally acknowledged, that a single man in possession of a good fortune, must be in want of a wife. (*Pride & Prejudice,* Jane Austen)

Happy families are all alike; every unhappy family is unhappy in its own way. (*Anna Karenina,* Leo Tolstoy)

 It was a bright cold day in April, and the clocks were striking thirteen. (*1984,* George Orwell)

Whether I shall turn out to be the hero of my own life, or whether that station will be held by anybody else, these pages must show. (*David Copperfield,* Charles Dickens)

It was a wrong number that started it, the telephone ringing three times in the dead of night, and the voice on the other end asking for someone he was not. (*City of Glass,* Paul Auster)

continues

Famous First Lines (Continued)

Through the fence, between the curling flower spaces, I could see them hitting. (*The Sound and the Fury*, William Faulkner)

The sky above the port was the color of television, tuned to a dead channel. (*Neuromancer*, William Gibson)

I had the story, bit by bit, from various people, and, as generally happens in such cases, each time it was a different story. (*Ethan Frome*, Edith Wharton)

He was an old man who fished alone in a skiff in the Gulf Stream and he had gone eighty-four days now without taking a fish. (*The Old Man and the Sea*, Ernest Hemmingway)

It was love at first sight. (*Catch 22*, Joseph Heller)

In my younger and more vulnerable years my father gave me some advice that I've been turning over in my mind ever since. (*The Great Gatsby*, F. Scott Fitzgerald)

"Where's papa going with that axe?" said Fern to her mother as they were setting the breakfast table. (*Charlotte's Web*, EB White)

Mr. and Mrs. Dursley of four, Privet Drive, were proud to say they were perfectly normal, thank you very much. (*Harry Potter and the Sorcerer's Stone*, JK Rowling)

All children, except one, grow up. (*Peter Pan*, JM Barrie)

The man in black fled across the desert, and the gunslinger followed. (*The Gunslinger*, Stephen King)

Detailed Description

Adding detail to description, a visualization group exercise of five groups, four in each:

1. Each student picks a favorite small physical object.
2. Each student then closes their eyes and focuses it clearly in their mind.
3. Each student jots down a list of physical details of the object.
4. Now, in turn, each student describes his or her object to the group.
5. Listeners jot down details of description.
6. Listeners close their eyes. Can they see the object?
7. Listeners check their list of details. What further information is needed to see the object clearly? The color? The size? The shape? The substance?
8. Each listener asks one question in turn until all can "see" the object clearly.
9. Now shift to the next student and begin at step four again.
10. Repeat until all students have described an object.

Once this process is complete, each group picks their favorite object and shares that description with the class.

Making a reader "see" a person or a scene or an object in your story is every writer's goal. The secret of that "seeing" often lies in the specificity and amount of detail a writer provides in his story. The more detail, the sharper the reader's focus. Another way to develop detail is using sensory perception. The following exercises help you to develop this ability.

Sketch Artist Exercise

Choose either a photo of someone you know or a photo in some publication to bring with you to the next class session. Get with a partner and, without showing your photo, imagine that the person is either missing or wanted for a crime, and you are the only person who can give an accurate description of what this person looks like. Describe for your partner as accurately and detailed as possible what this person looks like. While you describe, your partner should either draw or list the attributes that you mention. Your partner may also question you about details that are too ambiguous. For example, your character may have blonde hair, but what shade of blonde? Is it sandy blonde? Golden blonde? Platinum?

After you have finished describing, reveal your photo to your partner. How accurate was your description? What information would have been helpful for your partner to get a better visualization of the person in your photo?

Now exchange roles with your partner to find out how accurately he or she can describe the person in his or her photo. Follow with a free write to explain what details were missing and how you can use description to give your reader a better image of people, places, and things you mention in your personal narrative.

Five Senses Exercise

You might have heard someone say that in good writing, "your words paint a picture for the reader." However, an essay that leaves a lasting impression goes beyond that—it engages readers by giving them a feeling of "being there" in the picture. Including descriptions of the physical sense impressions in your writing will help your reader understand what it feels like to be in your shoes—even if those shoes are uncomfortable and smelly. Think about your narrative experience in relation to these five senses:

1. <u>Sight</u>—Most times we store away "images" in our minds of particular events in our lives. Because sight leaves such a strong impression with us, it is sometimes the easiest sense to recall. Also, it is a sense overwhelmingly presented through media: photos, home videos, magazine clippings. It is also an "immediate" sense—a loud bang may be caused by a number of things, but seeing a heavy book fall from a table to the floor will let you know that the sound was not the result of an exploding tire.

2. <u>Sound</u>—The pervasion of film in our culture makes us very aware of musical reinforcement of narrative; for example, "the-shark-is-coming" *Jaws* soundtrack. But have you ever thought of what the soundtrack of your life would sound like? Would it be filled with head-banging rock music or the melodic croon of a cello? Would there be no music at all, just a series of stomps and crashes? Sound gives us an impression of the pace of an environment—quiet and peaceful or loud and chaotic?

3. <u>Smell</u>—William Shakespeare wrote: "What's in a name? That which we call a rose by any other name would smell as sweet." But how sweet is that smell? Can it be as sweet as candy, or fruit, or even another flower like an orchid? Is one thing "sweeter" than the other? Does a wilting rose smell the same as a rose that has been freshly picked? How about a rose bush? (What the heck was Shakespeare talking about?)

4. <u>Touch</u>—Think about picking fruit while shopping at the supermarket. Before you purchase an apple, you may press it gently with your fingers. Why? Because touch tells you a lot about something. A firm apple tells you that it is fresh, while a mushy apple tells you that you might want to shop elsewhere. Like sound, touch can also give you an impression of an environment's pace or mood. Haven't you wondered why you sit in a comfortable, cushioned chair in a doctor's office instead of a hard wooden bench?

5. <u>Taste</u>—Unless you are writing about food, taste plays a small part in descriptive writing. However, when used appropriately, it can add "spice" to your writing.

Now think about your personal narrative experience. Is there any point where description coming from one or more of the five senses can enhance and develop your scene or character or action? For instance, "my grandfather smelled funny" is vague, "but my grandfather smelled like leather polish" is very specific and also tells us something about the man's possible work or hobbies. Pick a line from your narrative that describes a person (or scene, etc.) and develop it further by using sensory description.

Outdoor Description Exercise

This exercise may be used as an outdoor activity with the whole class or as a homework assignment.

Choose an outdoor location either near the classroom or of your choice if this is a homework assignment. Take a few moments to absorb some of the sensory details around you and write a paragraph describing the things you see, feel, hear, smell, and taste. Consider where you are seated. Are you sitting on the grass? A chair? A bench? What does it feel like? Are there people, animals, or buildings in your view? What do they look like? What scents can you detect in the air? Does it smell like spring or fall? What scents indicate those differences? What about sounds? Are there cars? People laughing? Animals scurrying? Can you taste anything? Do the things you smell influence the taste in your mouth?

Out on the Town
A homework exercise for the Personal Narrative

1. Pick a public place to visit. Libraries, cafeterias, student unions, restaurants, etc. will all work.
2. When you are at your destination, have a seat and observe what is going on around you.
3. Choose one person or one object, and based only on what you see, create a story, using as many sensory details as possible (sight, sound, smell, touch, taste). You want a person reading this narrative to know what it was like to sit in the public place that you chose.

From Vague to Detailed

Your rough draft is done, you've met the page requirements, and you think you are ready to print your paper and turn it in. Or are you? Will readers know what your story sounded like, smelled like, felt like, tasted like, and looked like? Will they see what you saw? Feel what you felt? There are two processes that can help you in making this the best paper it can be.

1. Have you looked at your sentences yet? Chances are that there are some sentences that need a little something extra to better convey what it was like to be you in that moment in time. It can be daunting to look at your paper, sentence by sentence, to revise it, but that examination can make the difference between a good paper and a great paper. What you need to do now is to go through and find the vague sentences, sentences that are boring or plain or colorless. And then add detail to them. Try this for at least three sentences in your paper. Your readers will be glad you did.

2. Exchange papers with a partner in class. Your job, and your partner's, is first to locate and circle all the vague single descriptive words in each other's paper. Share the results and then help each other to find more specific replacement words that better fit what you are trying to say in each case. For example: "The car crashed into the tree" can become "The dark green convertible crashed into the tree." Or, "The player dived over the line and into the end zone" can turn into "the short, stocky fullback dived over the line and into the end zone."

Think about the stories you have enjoyed reading, the specific descriptions that helped you as a reader to see the story more vividly. Try to reproduce that kind of description in your narrative.

Dialogue

Using dialogue, having characters speak directly to each other, makes them and your narrative come alive. But writing dialogue is never easy. And student writers even have problems incorporating dialogue correctly into their texts. Practice doesn't necessarily make perfect, but it certainly helps.

Rewriting

The final step of the generic writing process, the one that "polishes" the piece, is rewriting, or (re)vision, that (re)seeing of your paper made possible by critical response from readers. In this case, those readers are always your peers and your teacher. Sometimes those responses come in a chronological order that requires you, the writer, to produce three drafts: several classmates respond to your first, or rough, draft by answering a series of questions about the assignment that tell you, from a reader's viewpoint, what works and doesn't work in your paper.

Then you, as writer, can accept or reject the response suggestions for improvement. The goal of public writing—and each of the six formal assignments in this course is public writing—is to communicate your meaning to your reader. Obviously, then you want to

- rewrite any sentence or paragraph that readers find unclear or confusing,
- remove any material that is irrelevant to your paper's topic and focus,
- add any material necessary to explain a point or develop an idea or a character, etc.

For example, if a reader's summary of a paragraph in your paper does not reflect what you thought you were saying in that paragraph, your writing is unclear or confusing for that reader. What you do to rewrite that paragraph depends on the specific problem or what specifically the reader misunderstood. Sometimes you need to define more clearly the terms you are using because the reader is operating with a different set of definitions. Most often you need to add more explanation of a situation or more details about a person because the reader has insufficient information to clearly follow your paper. These errors, or content gaps, occur often in inexperienced writers' work because they already know the entire story in their heads. When they read over their writing, they automatically and often unconsciously "fill in" those gaps mentally for themselves. In this scenario, the writers cannot "see" the content gaps because, for them, they don't exist. This "spotting" of the problem is what writers need readers for. Occasionally you may need to delete material that doesn't belong in that paragraph because it is confusing and/or distracting the reader from the point you are trying to make.

In every instance, the final decision to accept or reject peer response rests with you, the writer. It is your paper, always.

Peer Response for Paper #1, the Personal Narrative:

Peer Response Sheet

Writer:_____ Reader:_____

1. Is the opening clear? Is it complete? Is it interesting? Does the opening provide a background without making it a preview of the paper to come (e.g., "I'm going to talk about . . .")? Make any suggestions to improve the opening here.
2. Please evaluate the closing. Does it do a nice job of wrapping up the paper without being a repetition only? Make any suggestions to improve the closing.
3. Is the paper organized? Do all the paragraphs connect to the opening and to each other? Make any suggestions here to improve the organization. Any paragraphs or passages out of place? Are any missing? Should any be added? If so, where? Should any be removed? Which one(s)? Indicate areas in the paper itself.
4. Does the writer fully develop his/her experience? Does he/she provide sufficient details? If so, circle an example or two of the details. If not, indicate a passage where the author needs to develop more detail.
5. Are the descriptions clear? Can you "see" the people, scene, or object being described? If so, mark a passage you feel works particularly well. If not, mark a passage that needs to be explained more.
6. Do you understand the "so what" of the personal experience the writer describes? Do you understand *how* that experience changed the writer's life? Make any suggestions about the clarity of the meaning of the experience here.
7. Mark any passages that you particularly like or that are really well-written by underlining them with **straight** lines.
8. Mark any passage that confuses you or is badly-written by underlining with **wavy** lines.
9. Take time to address the concerns the writer indicated with the free write on the back of this paper.
10. If there is time, list any serious mechanical or grammatical errors you notice at the end or in the text of the paper. **DO NOT CORRECT THEM!!!** For example, circle misspelled words but do not write in the correct spelling, or indicate where you feel punctuation should go but do not put in the mark itself.

Once you have your peer response and have rewritten the first narrative to produce a second draft, your teacher will provide feedback on that second draft. Using that feedback, you then rewrite again and produce the third and final draft of this assignment.

Teachers may provide this second response in a number of ways:

- feedback to students workshopping their papers in class,
- one-on-one conferences in the classroom or the teacher's office,
- group conferences (2 or 3 students) in class or in the teacher's office, or
- electronic response to drafts submitted via email or Web-CT or Blackboard, etc.

When the third draft is complete and you have thoroughly proofread it and corrected any errors, you are ready to turn in that paper. But, before you do so, you need to complete the final post-writing step, reflecting and analyzing the process you employed to produce this paper. Remember that English 180 is a class focusing on writing processes as well as the products those processes produce. Every subsequent assignment in this course follows the same generic processes outlined in this chapter. But within that generic framework, there are individual processes each student follows, some consciously and others unconsciously. One of our goals in this class is to make students fully aware of their own individual writing processes. To accomplish this, we require that, after completing each assignment, students write an inclusive "process sheet" completing that assignment. The final assignment in this course, the case study of yourself as a writer, is based on these sheets plus the feedback you received during the semester. Here are the process questions for Paper #1 along with a student sample process sheet answering those questions.

English 180
Process Write for Paper #1

Please write about your writing process for Paper #1. This writing may be in the form of a letter or an essay—whichever is easier for you. Attached is an example. While you will not have to answer every single question, you should be able to write on several. Absolutely do **not** give me a list of answers to the prompt questions below. Please elaborate and provide details in your responses. Feel free to mix, match, and rearrange the following prompts as you see fit to help you write this.

1. Why did you choose this topic? Are you happy with your choice?

2. What did you want to accomplish with this paper *or* what was your purpose in writing it (other than that it was required)? Do you feel you accomplished that purpose?

3. In writing this paper, what helped you produce the final draft? Was the peer feedback helpful? Were the in-class discussions helpful? Did the examples from the book help? Did anyone else help you? If so, who was it and how did he/she/they help you?

4. When did you actually write this paper? Did you write it all at once or in parts? Where did you write it? Under what physical circumstances (e.g. standing or sitting, with or without music, with or without food, etc.)?

5. How long did the first draft take? Did the re-write take less time or more time? Was the re-write easier or harder to write than the first draft?

6. What do you like best about your paper? Least? Elaborate and show me.

7. What one thing would you do differently if you had the chance to do the paper over? Why?

Process Example

I really enjoyed writing this paper because it gave me an opportunity to share an important event in my life. When we were first assigned to write about something from our timeline, I was a little nervous. Most of the writing I have ever done in school was about a topic that was not important to me, so I was not too motivated to work too hard on it. This topic was different. I really cared about what I had to say because I wanted to show my reader how much the event meant to me and how devastating the event really was.

It was really easy for me to choose what event to write about, but writing the paper proved to be more difficult. It honestly took me two whole days to write a rough draft because every time I tried to write, my roommate would crank up the TV because she wanted to watch *Next*. I tried going to the study room on my floor, but too often people were in there playing poker and being loud. I found out I can write pretty well in the lab in the library, but I need to have some Kanye West playing to help me focus. Every hour or so, I would need to get up and stretch so my back wouldn't hurt too badly from sitting in those uncomfortable chairs. The first day I tried writing in the library, I forgot to get something to eat first so all I could think about was how hungry I was. On the second day I made sure I went to the cafe before I went to the library so I wouldn't be hungry.

I really enjoyed the peer responding activity we did in class. My responders offered me a lot of advice on how to improve my paper. The memoir by Bragg was helpful too because it showed me how a memoir could and should be. It showed me that—unlike how I was taught to write in high school—you don't have to tell everything in your introduction or review everything in your conclusion. Your tips and little talks helped out a lot too, thanks!

Rewriting my paper was a lot harder than I thought it would be. I thought that all I would have to do is fix everything my responders said and I would be done. However, there were a few things they suggested that would have totally changed what I wanted to say. I asked my best friend what he thought and he said I should just leave it, so I did. Because of the visualization exercise in class, I really tried to make sure I had plenty of specific details in my paper. That is what I am probably most proud of. When I described the accident, I changed a lot of the verbs and added adjectives to make the event more realistic. I also went from writing about the entire accident to the moment when my life flashed before my eyes and I saw how excited I was on my 7th birthday when I got my first bike. I still have trouble with using commas, but I hope to get better over the year.

If I had to do this assignment over, I think I would have chosen a more specific topic when I started. Writing about an accident in detail takes a lot of space and time. In my first draft I covered all the events of the accident, but I felt I could have a better job of being more detailed. In my revision, I tried to be more detailed. It would have been a lot easier to do this if I had been more focused the first time.

Part Three
The Reflection Paper

ASSIGNMENT TWO: The Reflection Paper

Self reflection sounds complicated, difficult, and even scary, but in reality it is a simple process of self-analysis, something we already do every day unconsciously and consciously. In terms of thinking in general, *The Oxford English Dictionary* defines reflection as "meditating on," "thinking about," "considering," or "reminding oneself." In terms of this second writing assignment, we are asking you to think carefully about the event you chose to narrate in Paper #1, to examine in depth why this event was so important to you, and to explain why you chose to write about it in the first place. In other words, you are analyzing your own writing to discover what that event meant to you, what you learned from it, and how it affected the rest of your life. Here you are examining your personal experience in order to place it within a larger social, cultural, or ethical framework by asking yourself a series of questions:

1. Why did this event matter so much to me?
2. Why did I choose to write about it?
3. How did this event change my life?
4. What did I learn from this event that I can share profitably with others?
5. What else did I learn from writing about the event?
6. What would readers learn from reading my personal narrative?

Answering these questions enables you to analyze your own experience as you recorded it in your personal narrative. And when you analyze your experience on both these personal and universal levels, you are *reflecting* on that experience in terms of its relevance to your life and the lives of others. You are also mastering, on a basic level, the essential skill of analysis that you must learn to succeed now in your college classes and eventually in your future career.

Remember that the assignments in this course are deliberately sequenced in order of increasing sophistication and difficulty so that students can use what they learned in each preceding paper to help them write the next one. Therefore, the reflection, based on the personal narrative, uses both skills learned in writing that narrative (writing openings, closing, dialogue, details) and actual material from the paper itself. Here a concise summary of the original narrative serves as an opening for the reflection paper and as the core text you analyze in depth as you reflect on the importance of this event on your individual life and try to place it in a universal context.

This kind of reflection is both difficult and complex because it requires students to engage in self analysis on several levels. Student writers need to determine

- the effects of their event on their lives,
- the effects of their writing about the event on them, and
- the effects on a reader reading their narratives.

Because this analysis is so in-depth, English 180 teachers have chosen to introduce it in one-on-one conferences with individual students. Using the final draft of Paper #1 as a launching pad, students discuss their original narratives in the light of summarizing them concisely and thoroughly while simultaneously analyzing them to discover their effects in both particular personal lives and the more general universal sphere. Conferences should help students identify relevant elements of the core event as well as discover ways to link individual lessons taught by the original narrative to more universal lessons applicable to audiences within and outside the English 180 classroom.

Just the act of reflection itself includes first remembering the event for yourself and then examining that event to discover its significance for you. Writing a reflection paper implies sharing both your reflection (the summary of the event) and its significance with other people. You invite others to share your experience *and* your analysis of it in hopes that they will learn from both as you did.

Prewriting:

> ### Freewriting Prompts for Reflective Writing
>
> - What was the easiest part of writing Paper #1? What was the hardest?
> - Why did you choose the topic you chose for Paper #1?
> - What did you learn from your experience?
> - What do you want others to learn from reading your paper?
> - What is your favorite movie? Or song? Or book? Or TV series? Why do you like it so much? What have you learned from it?
>
> Fun or just practice in reflection (remembering and analyzing for significance):
>
> - Write a eulogy for a family member, friend, or enemy.
> - Write a speech as Best Man for your brother or closest friend.
> - Write a speech as Maid of Honor for your sister or best friend.
>
> ### Freewrite Freeze
>
> Looking through your personal narrative, choose a favorite scene or moment. Now "freeze" that moment by taking a mental snapshot. Stand back and look at this snapshot as if it were a painting. What does it look like? What colors do you see? Are there any people in the picture? What do their expressions look like? What's in the background of the picture . . . the foreground? Are there any minute details that are barely noticeable?

The first step in writing the Reflective Paper is re-reading and summarizing the personal narrative. *Webster's* defines a summary as "a succinct statement of the principle points" while *Funk and Wagnall's* describes a summary as greatly condensed and concise. In this instance, the summary of the personal narrative should be brief, concise, and complete; it should cover all the relevant facts without the detailed embellishment that made the original narrative so effective. A two- or three-page narrative can easily be summarized in one-half to two-thirds page of the three-to-five-page reflective essay. To help students to accurately analyze and summarize the text of their narratives, an exercise in writing a generic summary is provided. Apply it to the original narrative:

Summary Process

Read the passage carefully. Determine its structure. Identify the author's purpose in writing. (This will help you distinguish between more important and less important information.)

Reread. This time divide the passage into sections or states of thought. The author's use of paragraphing will often be a useful guide. *Label*, on the passage itself, each section or stage of thought. *Underline* key ideas and terms.

Write a thesis, a one sentence summary, of the entire passage. The thesis should express the central idea of the passage as you have determined it from the preceding steps. You may find it useful to keep in mind the information contained in the lead sentence or paragraph of most newspaper stories—the who, what, when, where, why, and how of the matter. For persuasive passages, summarize in a sentence the author's conclusion. For descriptive passages, indicate the subject of the description and its key feature(s). Note: In some cases a *suitable thesis may already be in the original passage.* If so, you may want to quote it directly in your summary.

Write the first draft of your summary by (1) combining the thesis with your list of one sentence summaries or (2) combining the thesis with one sentence summaries *plus* significant details from the passage. In either case, eliminate repetition and less important information. Disregard minor details, or generalize them. Use as few words as possible to convey the main ideas.

Check your summary against the original passage, and make whatever adjustments are necessary for accuracy and completeness.

1. *Revise your summary*, inserting transitional words and phrases where necessary to ensure coherence. Check for style. *Avoid a series of short, choppy sentences.* Combine sentences for a smooth, logical flow of ideas. Check for grammatical correctness, punctuation, and spelling.

When writing summaries or any other kind of paper, "flow" is an important readability factor. As writers, you want to create one smooth, coherent piece, not a jerky, hard to follow collection of individual paragraphs. No matter how good those paragraphs might be, they must be connected to each other and to your central idea in order to form a single whole essay. The best papers read so smoothly that readers sometimes don't even notice the transitions, or connecting lengths, that bind the paper together.

The very best kind of these transitions is a logical transition, one that connects one paragraph with another through further development of content. For example, in a narrative, the chronological action often automatically links the paragraphs together in a chain of directly related events. In an expository paper or report, one paragraph might introduce, define and/or describe a particular topic the writer has chosen to write about, and the next paragraph might provide a single developed example or a list of examples illustrating that topic. By using this order, the writer creates a logical connection through the actual content of the two paragraphs. Or, in an argument paper, the second paragraph might provide evidence of an assertion made in the preceding paragraph, again creating that automatic content link. No transitional phrase or sentence is necessary in these cases.

But sometimes that kind of logical transition just doesn't work. In those cases writers need transitional words or phrases or even whole sentences to link paragraphs together so that the readers can easily follow the train of thought being developed by the writers. Depending on what kind of link a writer needs, the following words signal transitions:

When connecting ideas opposed to each other, use

Although	Nevertheless
But	Though
Despite	Whereas
Even if	While
However	Yet
In spite of	

When connecting linked or supporting ideas, use

Also	Indeed
As well	In fact
And	Moreover
Further	Similarly
Furthermore	: [colon]
In addition	; [semicolon]
Not only	. . . but also

When introducing a cause or a reason from previous statements, use

As	Because
For	Since
As a result of	Due to
On account of	

When introducing results or conclusions from previous statements, use

As a result	Therefore
Consequently	Thus
Hence	To sum up
In conclusion	In consequence
It follows that . . .	So

When introducing an example, use

For example	Such as
For instance	: [colon]
In that	

When introducing alternatives, use

Either . . . or	Neither . . . nor
If only	Rather than
Instead	Unless
Instead of	Whether . . . or
In that case	

When introducing the degree or extent of something, use

For the most part	To a certain extent
So . . . that	To some extent
Such . . . that	To some degree

When introducing comparisons or contrasts, use

By comparison	On the one hand
Conversely	On the other hand
In contrast	

Obviously writers have a variety of choices depending on their purpose and preference. Which choice they make within a category is strictly a personal stylistic decision. What matters is that they recognize the need for a transition within their text and then choose that transition from the appropriate category.

The following exercises will help you recognize that need and choose appropriately in your own writing.

Transition Activity

Transition sentences and phrases help your readers move from one paragraph to the next and from one idea to another. Think of transitions as important links that establish coherence in your essays, improving the "flow" and readability of your papers.

Exercise I

- Take a student or professional essay sample text that the class has not read, cut it up into paragraphs and number the paragraphs.
- Divide the class into groups of four or five people.
- Give one set of cut-up paragraphs to each group.
- Ask each group to arrange the paragraphs into a coherent essay.
- Share results with the whole class, discussing how groups determined the order of the paragraphs.
- In discussion, pick out transitional signals (sentences, phrases, or words) that connect the paragraphs.

Exercise II

- Individually, every student in the class writes one paragraph. This paragraph can be about absolutely anything: a daily occurrence, another person, an object, a thought or conviction, or an event. Feel free to write creatively; there are no rules to what you can or can't write about.
- Break down into groups of four people.
- In groups, share all four of your paragraphs aloud.
- The first challenge is to decide on the most sensible order the paragraphs should be organized in to form one essay. The paragraphs probably don't make much sense when put together, but that's okay—in fact they shouldn't make sense yet.
- Once each group reaches a consensus on the paragraph order, group members need to work together to formulate transition sentences to go between each paragraph, attempting to somehow connect the paragraphs' ideas and form one complete essay.
- The finished activity should look something like this:

  *Paragraph 1
  *Transition sentence
  *Paragraph 2
  *Transition sentence
  *Paragraph 3
  *Transition sentence
  *Paragraph 4

Conscious self-reflection is one of the most difficult meta-cognitive processes for students to master because it requires focus, concentration, and sophisticated analytical skills. Yet such reflection is essential for developing and extending consistent learning patterns in college and beyond. Successful critical thinking, so essential for informed, active citizens in the twenty-first century, requires the ability to reflect in-depth (meditate on, think about, try to analyze, etc.) about current events and societal problems as well as personal issues and relationships. Thus, cultivating this ability through writing involves much more than simply mastering a new assignment genre. A series of interactive classroom exercises can help develop this essential ability.

Reflection through Visual Memory
An activity for groups of two, three, or four people

Instructions for students:

1. Choose and bring to class a photograph that you appear in or have taken that has a strong significance for you in your life.
2. Switch photos with group members. Do not tell the rest of the group anything about the picture. Don't reveal who or what the picture consists of. Say nothing about the setting or people or background or context.
3. Once you have someone else's photo, freewrite on what you see in the photo, considering
    *What do you think is going on in the photo?
    *Where and when do you think it was taken?
    *What importance do you think the photo has for your classmate who gave it to you? Why did she/he choose this photo?
4. On a separate sheet of paper, freewrite on the significance this picture holds for you personally.
    *Does the subject of the photo remind you of anything that happened in your own life?
    *What emotions do you feel looking at the photo?
    *Does it stir up any memories of your own that you can associate with it?
    *Have you ever taken (or been the subject of) a similar photo?

Once you finish both freewrites, return the picture to its owner. Compare notes with that person. How close were your guesses involving the subject of the photo?
    *Were your own thoughts and memories similar to your classmates?
5. Record your findings.

When reflecting on a particular "life altering event," students often have difficulty making connections between their individual reflections and a more abstract level of universal human experience. A student has trouble, for example, realizing that moving into an apartment and living away from his/her parents for the first time is part of a larger, graduate "coming of age" process everyone goes through. But putting an individual's experience into a larger, universal context is one of the essential results of any successful, in-depth reflection. Critically thinking about the significance of the experience requires analyzing and understanding the significance of that experience both on the individual and universal levels. Again, interactive classroom activities can help students work through this all important process.

Further Reflection: The "What If" Game

You are now reflecting on the experience you chose to write about in your personal narrative assignment to determine what you learned from that experience and what others can learn from reading about it. Playing the "What If" game can help you to determine both the significance of your experience and its relation to the big picture or larger more encompassing universal human experience. This is an individual exercise students should do at their desks and then share afterwards.

- Take a minute and close your eyes.
- Try to imagine what your life would be like today if that event (the experience your wrote about in Paper #1) had never happened.
- Think about all the ways you believe it changed your life, who you are, and how you see the world.

But what if that event had never happened?

For example, what if that event had made you afraid of something, what would your life be like today if you were not afraid of that something?

Take out a sheet of paper, ask yourself the following series of questions, prefacing each one with the phrase

What if ____ had not happened?"

- Would I still be here at WIU right now?
- Would I have the same friends I have today?
- Would I dress the way I do now, look the way I do to others?
- Would I be majoring in the same thing?
- Would I still have the same relationship with my parents? My girlfriend/boyfriend/best friend?
- Would I still believe in the same values (religious, work ethic, political etc.)?
- Would I still want the things I want now?

Write down the answer to each question. Add any other questions you feel might help you see the personal and universal importance of the experience.

The final activity in this prewriting stage is analyzing another's self reflective experience. The best venue for such an analysis is a visual one like television because students are already familiar with both the medium and many of the individual series you could use for this activity. Four very popular sitcoms—*Everybody Hates Chris, My Name Is Earl, Dougie Howser, M.D.,* and *The Wonder Years*—all employ self reflective narration in every episode. Choose one, pick an episode, let the class view it, and then answer the following questions together in class:

Generic questions about self reflective narratives from a TV series:

1. Can you relate to anything in the video and make connections to your own experiences or stories you've heard after watching it?
2. What problems do characters face and how do they overcome them (if they do)?
3. Do characters in the video make decisions that can or will affect them or the people around them in the future? If so, what were they and what do they say about the character making the decision and the world in general?
4. Does anything in the video relate to historical or social movements?
5. How is conflict or change handled in the video?
6. Why do characters act the way they do? What is their possible motivation?
7. What did you learn or could others learn from the video?
8. Why would others want to watch the video, or why is it important?
9. What social, cultural, moral, or ethical problems does the video address?

Reflection Readings and Other Texts:

Stephen King's "The Body"
Film *Stand By Me*
TV series *The Wonder Years* (any episode)
Bell Hooks "Straightening Out Hair"
Chanrithy Him "When Broken Glass Floats"
Tim O'Brien "The Things They Carried"
Tillie Olsen "I Stand here Ironing"

Again, to help students visualize what a reflection assignment looks like when successfully completed, here are two sample papers:

Reflection on Making the Cut
By Jackson Courter

Not much was visually different about cut night. My teammates and I ran lazily through simple passing and shooting drills in the gloomy space of the Edison Elementary School gym as a young coach's assistant looked on, half-supervising us. This scene could have been taken from any weeknight practice in the last thirty days, but on this particular night everyone's attention was fixed on the door to the locker room. Everyone wondered what would be said on the other side of the door when it was their turn to hear the official word on whether they made the eighth-grade basketball team or not. I was on the bubble, not sure if the coaches would keep me or cut me, not even sure if I wanted to remain on the team, since I wouldn't get much playing time if I did. Perhaps, if I made the cut, I would decide not to play on the team that season and, instead, practice on my own, hoping to return my freshman year with a sharpened skill set.

When my turn finally came, I tried not to smile too profoundly when Coach Clauson told me "You are one of the guys we're going to keep." Then he said I wouldn't see much playing time, but encouraged me to keep training hard. He didn't reiterate the offer he made a few nights earlier to bubble players, that we could voluntarily withdraw from the team if we didn't want to stay, though I knew it still applied—I had only to turn in my preseason jersey at the end of practice. For a moment, as I walked back on the court, I couldn't make up my mind, but then I looked at the team, remembering that these guys were my friends; I didn't want to walk out on them, and, more importantly, they didn't want to see me go. So, when Steve, my best friend and teammate, asked me if I was going to stay, I found myself saying yes.

After practice, as I walked through the biting breeze of mid-November to my dad waiting in our van, I realized that no uncertainty ever truly existed about whether I would stay or not. Even though I truly had to choose to stay, that choice was inevitable—I had been committed ever since I decided to try out for the team in the first place. I knew that if I wanted to prove to myself and to others that I had what it took to be on the team, I needed to stay for the whole season—I could sense that the unspoken rule was that making the cut and quitting didn't legitimately count as "making it." I couldn't nullify my struggle to make the cut by just walking away.

Five years later, eighth-grade basketball seems distant and trivial. Nobody cares anymore about that season, who was on the team, who got playing time, who was the most talented, or who worked the hardest. I'm not a different man because of the experience. I wouldn't be living a completely different lifestyle if I hadn't chosen to try out for the team. Nonetheless, the experience helped me come to terms with the deeper meanings of struggle. I learned that struggle is a universal concept that doesn't rely on time, place, age, or activity. I can relate that struggle from five years ago, the desperation I felt during it, and the triumph I felt after it, to numerous struggles I have had since eighth grade.

continues

Reflection on Making the Cut (Continued)

The most severe of these struggles came in my senior year of high school, a grueling period in which I was forced to handle the overwhelming pressure of two AP classes, decide which university I would attend, and write application essays for scholarships. During these trials, I drew on my fight to make the cut for inspiration to grind through that year without letting up, without giving in to my longing to drop my AP classes and submit to senioritis. I knew that if I persevered, at the end of the year I would emerge a tougher, more focused person, just as I had after disciplining myself to make the team and stay with it for the rest of the season. After my senior year, when I learned that I had received A's in all my classes, nearly all the scholarships I had applied for, a perfect score on my final AP English portfolio, and the highest possible score on the AP European History test, I experienced the same pride and elation that I did five years ago when I heard that I had made the team.

The circumstances of the two struggles were completely different. In eighth grade, I had to endure burning muscles and hours of repetitive practice each day. In my senior year, I had to will myself through countless late nights to complete innumerable assignments and read hundreds of pages of text. However, the willpower that each effort required was the same—both times I relied on the same fighting spirit, the same will to achieve the highest possible goal.

It would be unreasonable to say that making the cut and sticking with the team transformed me into an overachiever or gave me an imperishable iron will. But that experience came at a very formative time in my adolescence, and my choice to do the hard thing, to choose discipline over mediocrity and laziness, set a constructive tone for my development and helped me see the power and self-esteem that achievement could bring me. It revealed to me the equation that dictates much of life, that more struggle now equals more reward later.

Let It Out
Sarah Brynda
Reflection Paper

I have never been good at sharing my feelings and expressing my emotions. If there ever is a problem, I have to be the one to fix it and make sure everyone else is ok. If I disregard my feelings, then I'll be ok and not have to deal with anything, especially if I keep myself as occupied as possible. After almost twenty years of marriage, my parents decided to get a divorce. Instead of dealing with all the change taking place in my family, I focused on graduation, going to college and my boyfriend. I tried to be normal and happy; I had all these great things going on. I kept asking myself: so what if my parents are getting divorced? Fifty percent of marriages end up that way, so it's not like I was the first to experience it. If I rationalized my feelings, it wouldn't hurt so much. But my Dad and I have always been very close. Having him move out was going to change my life completely; my family was never going to be the same. No one talked about it. They acted like he was going on some extended vacation and he'd be back soon. What I really needed was to talk to someone about what was going on in my life.

My Dad moved out in March. I went with him to his new house the day he finally left. He packed his truck with a few things he'd need until the movers came. He left first, with me closely following in my car, because of course I wasn't going to live where he was. The drive there was hard; all I could think of was all the memories we had as a family. I thought about vacations, parties, family nights with pizza and games, my little brother coming home, pets we'd all had, and how my Dad was there for all of it. Now he wasn't. We'd have to make new memories when I got to visit.

When we pulled up, I was a little disappointed, because I thought the house would have been better. It could have been a mansion, and I still would have thought it wasn't good enough. We unpacked everything quickly, even though half of the things could wait, but that way we could focus on the task in front of us, instead of how we were really feeling. After all the unpacking was done, we had a nice dinner together and talked about everything but what was going on. Finally, it was time for me to leave. We hugged, said goodbye and that we'd see each other soon. We never once cried in front of each other. As soon as I pulled away, and left my Dad all alone, in his new house, to start his new life, I lost it. I have never cried that hard, but I wasn't crying for myself. I was crying for my Dad and how hard things were going to be for him alone.

My Dad moved out almost two years ago. Yet I still get upset thinking about that day and how hard it was to leave him. I still haven't dealt with my feelings. I cried while I was writing this, but for the same reasons as when I left. It hurts to think of him all alone, in an empty house. I know that I need to deal with my feelings, but I am afraid that once I open up, I'm never going to stop or that the same hurt is going to come back. It was too painful the first time, and I never want to experience it again. I only made matters worse by rationalizing my feelings. Telling myself that divorce is common and that I shouldn't sit around feeling sorry only made things worse. If something upsets you, you should deal with it. Even if it's something as trivial as seeing a squished bug on the sidewalk. If it matters to you, it's important, and should be dealt with.

An experience like this is especially difficult for a person who isn't good at dealing with change. I am one of those people. My mom bought me a new comforter for my bed when I was eight. I hated it. It wasn't my bed anymore so I slept on the couch for a month. Then, we got a new couch, and it was back to my bed. Instead of dealing with the pain and feelings, I either run away or blame someone. In this case, I blamed my Mom for making my life change. I felt that everything that was happening was her fault. I felt that she took the easy way out; instead of working on their problems, she ran away. I hated her for a long time, and I wasn't very nice to her. I didn't even buy her anything for Mother's Day. I didn't feel like she deserved a special day to celebrate what a wonderful mother she is, because in my head she had ruined my life and our family.

I've grown up a little since then, and forgiven her. I no longer have that immature mentality that she ruined my life. I realized that their problems didn't have anything to do with me. If they thought they could be happier apart, then why not let them be happy? Otherwise you end up like me. I never dealt with my pain, and I am paying for it now. Whenever my boyfriend and I fight, I either blame him for everything, or run away before it gets too tough. He wants to talk it out like a rational person should, but all I do is end up yelling and picking on him; instead of the issue that caused the fight. I know why I am the way I am; I buried everything that happened with my parents and never dealt with the changes. Now all of my emotions are trying to escape, but in a different way; one that is causing more problems in my life.

If you think you are too tough to deal with your emotions, you are wrong. You need to talk about what you are feeling with other people; it can only help you. Otherwise, one single event in your life can set a precedent for how you handle every situation.

continues

Let It Out (*Continued*)
Sarah Brynda
Reflection Paper

I have a friend who dated a girl for almost three years. Then, one day, she ended it. She wasn't very good to him. She would cut him off in every argument and never let him get to say his side. He did everything for her, yet got nothing in return. I didn't know this friend while he dated that girl, but I can see that what he went through is how he handles every situation now. He never let out any of his anger towards her. Now, if there's an argument with someone, he runs away, and never talks about it. Also, at times he can be the most generous person, but then when he needs something, it's like well I did this, this and this for you, so you owe me this favor. My friend and I are very much the same way, and often bump heads. We can be the best of friends, but when one little thing happens, neither of us wants to deal with it. One day, we talked about a particular argument that we had. He told me that while he was yelling, then storming off, I wasn't me; I was his ex-girlfriend.

You don't want to be like that. Look back at past events in your life and see if you are still doing them today. You don't want to get into a pattern of the same behavior. It will only cause more problems with those around you.

Writing

Once you have thoroughly analyzed your narrative and discovered its significance on a personal and universal level, you are ready to write the first draft of Paper #2.

Paper #2: The Reflective Essay

Assignment

Paper #1, the Personal Narrative, will be rewritten/(re)envisioned into Paper #2, the Reflective Essay

In this new paper, no more than two-thirds of a page, or 1 page should contain the actual personal experience you wrote about in Paper #1. This is because the experience of Paper #1 serves as the starting point for Paper #2.

Therefore, the first step in this rewrite will be to summarize and condense to a tighter, shorter version the experience in Paper #1.

This is a shift from "showing" readers a particular experience, person, or place to thinking about and exploring a larger meaning of that experience for you and your readers.

- Now your primary concern is "Why does this experience matter (to you and to the world at large)?" Do other people have similar experiences in different ways? Can you think of some sort of analogy for your story?
- You can address readers directly and open with an "I/You" link.
- The tone of the essay can be conversational and informal.

Possibilities and Points

Explore the experience in relation to:

- Social problems and customs
- Virtues and vices
- Morality
- Hopes and fears, or other emotional issues
- Childhood concepts
- Coming of Age experiences of other "rites of passage"

Rationale:

The point is to discover not just what this experience means to you (that may have been the conclusion to your first paper) but to learn what this kind of experience means to people in general, what it says about human nature, of the world we live in, etc. This is the analytical aspect of the experience rather than the experience itself.

Ask yourself the question, so what? Why does my experience matter—to me, or to others? What are the larger issues at stake, the general "lessons" others can learn from reading my narrative?

*****

Fact Finding and the Universal Experience

Now that your reflection paper is well on its way toward completion, it is time for you to complete the last part of the assignment, connecting your experience with the wider range of human experience in general. Even though your experience may seem unique to you, chances are that many others in the world have experienced a similar event in their lives. And you will need to prove that universal connection in your reflection paper.

To make that connection, you will need to include one or two facts that link your experience to the large human experience. Go to the university library's reference desk and ask the librarian to help you find some facts relating to your paper. Don't worry about citations or formal research at this point; just locate the material you need and mention it in your paper to cement this required connection.

Brainstorming for Material

You have summarized your personal narrative and are now ready to write the major portion of Paper #2, your actual reflection about the experience. Brainstorming is a technique that helps generate material for any paper. This brainstorming exercise is focused specifically on your reflection assignment.

Where the personal narrative ends, reflection begins . . .

The Reflective Essay encourages you to explore your experience in relation to social problems and customs . . . like virtues and vices, morality, hopes, fears, emotional issues, and ethical problems. In reflective writing, the topic or focus of your paper is not always the same as it is in your narrative essay. The topic of your reflective essay is what something means from your narrative essay. Try to go beyond the normal, common associations—add your own twist, your own significance. Use your own imagination, creativity, and originality to "own your idea."

Beginning to Brainstorm about the Reflective Essay

1. Out of all the events you could have chosen to write about, why did you pick this particular event?
2. What was it about this particular event that meant or mattered so much to you that you chose to write about it?
3. How or in what way did the events you wrote about change your life? What impact did they have on who you are today?
4. What did you learn from this event that you can share with others?
5. How is this event similar to experiences that other people have had in their lifetimes?
6. Use your brainstorming techniques. Do a free write or make a list of ideas for your reflective essay. Think about people, places, things, objects, events. (See Chapter 4, pgs. 136–139 for examples!)

The following chart is an example of the way you can pair up individual incidents of your personal experience narrative with lessons learned through reflecting on those original incidents.

General Topic: Camping and Biking Trip			
Action #1	Action #2	Action #3	Action #4
Gearing up	First sight of the Missouri River	Finding a place to rest	First night of camping
Lesson Learned	Lesson Learned	Lesson Learned	Lesson Learned
Planning ahead is the most important thing when setting off on any type of adventure. Without preparing properly, real problems can occur and turn a fun experience into a disaster.	I thought of all the people throughout time who have traveled this same route and how the sight that I was enjoying was seen by so many and so long ago. Also, I thought about how the world has changed so much, but this great river has remained relatively the same.	People are generally good and decent. We often grow up learning to be wary of other people when in fact most are helpful and willing to stick their neck out for you, regardless of whether they know you or not.	Sleeping under the stars is incredibly peaceful. All the noises of nature appear as a lullaby.

To help pair up the incidents in your paper, you should fill in the following blank chart in the same way the previous example did but using your own incidents and reflections. This will give you a basic outline for the initial body paragraphs of your paper.

General Topic:			
Action #1	Action #2	Action #3	Action #4
Lesson Learned	Lesson Learned	Lesson Learned	Lesson Learned

Focus on Meaning

Now that you have your material, focus on the meaning of your experience on a more universal level. You are moving away from the experience that you have summarized toward a larger, more universal level, the topic of your reflection, the <u>so what</u> of the experience for yourself and others. Now is the time to start making those generalizations about your experience, to discuss how it relates to others and society in general.

- Start by making connections between the <u>past</u> event and the <u>present</u> moment.
- Organize your writing to move from the concrete (your experience) towards the abstract (its universal message for others).
- Use a reflective tone—be tentative, thoughtful, and questioning: invite readers to share in your reflection—the I/You link works well here.
- Lead up to (write your way towards) the universal meaning or connection or lesson you have discovered in your reflective processes and want to share with your readers.
- That universal lesson or connection or meaning and its possible application for readers makes an effective conclusion.

Workshopping

During the drafting process, students will spend one class period working on drafts in class while the teacher circulates and provides help with

Introductions
Conclusions
Organization
Transitions
Shift from Specific to General

(Re)Vision Strategies

The process of revision is something few beginning writers understand. They think revision is proofreading to find and correct the mechanical errors in their papers—the misspelled words, faulty punctuation, grammar mistakes, etc. But proofreading is only one stage, the last and often least important stage, of revision. Real (re)vision is a (re)seeing of your paper, looking at it from different angles, and, with the help of peer and/or teacher feedback, changing that paper in major ways. Such revision might include adding material where it is needed, eliminating material that is repetitious or unnecessary or irrelevant, reorganizing and restructuring whole paragraphs or sentences within paragraphs, moving material to other parts of the paper, or even totally changing your introduction or conclusion. These massive changes deal with the content and organization of your paper, not the mechanics covered by proofreading. And there is no point in proofreading first because you will be wasting time correcting errors that will often disappear in your revised text. Proofreading is always the *last* step of revision, what you do when you have completed the revised draft of your assignment.

(Re)Vision: Seeing Again from a Different Perspective

"How can I know what I think until I see what I say?"—E.M. Forster

"All good writing is rewriting."—Unknown Writing Teacher

Hopefully you are revising with the help of teacher and/or peer feedback. Always take their comments into consideration throughout all parts of the revision process. There are two ways to look at revision:

- One classifies two kinds of rewriting—MACRO-REVISION & MICRO-REVISION
- The other divides it into three stages—ACTUAL REVISION, EDITING, PROOFREADING

Actually both can be combined logically to provide beginning writers with a clear, chronological blueprint for revising a paper—in other words, what to do and when (in what order) to do it.

Stage one can be labeled MACRO-REVISION and includes the actual (re)visioning or reworking of the paper's approach, content, and organization. It should always be the first step in the overall revision process. It involves the essay as a whole and the paragraphs that compose it.

Here the writer asks these kinds of questions:

1. Did I approach the subject from the right angle? Will a different approach better accomplish what I'm trying to do here?
2. Are my points arranged in the best possible order to say what I am trying to say? Would rearranging any of them make my paper clearer? Better organized? More effective?
3. What did I leave out that I need to complete, support, or explain my subject and/or position in this paper? Is there a major point I forgot or minor evidence I need to include for such a point?
4. Did I explain each point fully so it will be clear to my reader? Can a reader follow my reasoning, connect my points and relate them to my controlling idea (thesis)? Have I left a "content gap" a reader might not be able to fill in?
5. Is there anything in the paper that shouldn't be there—something unrelated to the idea I am developing, a digression that should be eliminated?
6. Is my introduction effective? Would it make someone want to read this paper?
7. Is my conclusion complete? Did it go too far? Not far enough?

Obviously these are in-depth questions that require (re)seeing the paper—what it says and how it says it as well as what it doesn't (but maybe should) say. This stage is MACRO-REVISION because it requires major rewriting and reworking of the paper's content and organization and maybe even its approach or point of view.

The second two stages are MICRO-REVISION or EDITING and PROOFREADING, in exactly that order.

EDITING, stage two, includes the sentence level of the paper rather than the whole essay or its paragraphs. EDITING has two purposes:

1. Clarifying content
2. Improving style

There are two questions to ask here:

1. Does each sentence stay what you want it to say?
2. Is there a more effective and efficient way for that sentence to say what you want it to say?

Hints:
1. Replace passive voice if it is possible without changing the meaning of your sentence.
2. Avoid jargon, slang, or unnecessarily big words. Be clear.

3. Express ideas concisely. Eliminate unnecessary words and phrases. Less really is more.
4. Vary your sentences in length and structure. Don't write every sentence in subject-verb-object order.
5. Use parallel constructions for parallel ideas.

PROOFREADING is the second stage of MICRO-REVISION and the last stage of revising. It includes checking for surface errors in grammar, spelling, and punctuation and eliminating them. To do so, complete the following steps:

1. Read the paper aloud.
2. Ask someone else to read it for those three kinds of errors.
3. Don't assume spell check caught anything.
4. Never use a grammar check. None on the market can read for context and they will mess up your paper.
5. Use the required text, *A Pocket Style Manual,* for grammar and punctuation questions.

Revision is essential for all good writing. No paper is carved in stone. It's yours and you can make any and all changes necessary to improve it and make it the best possible piece of writing.

Peer responding provides feedback essential for your successful revision; readers always catch mistakes and omissions that writers overlook in their own texts.

Peer Responding Sheet

Questions you would like the editors to answer or things you would like them to look for:

1. Is the paper organized? Do all the paragraphs connect to the intro? To each other?
2. Is the summary portion of the paper complete? Do you understand what the person's experience was? Did they leave anything out that you wonder about? Is it one page or less of the entire paper?
3. Do you understand why the person's experience mattered to him or her? Do you understand how it relates to a larger world issue?
4. Are there any paragraphs or passages out of place? Are any missing? Should any be added? If so, where? Should any be removed? Which one(s)? Indicate areas in the paper itself.
5. Mark any passage you particularly like or that is really well written by underlining it with <u>straight</u> lines.
6. Mark any passage that confuses you by underlining it with <u>wavy</u> lines.
7. If there is time, list any serious mechanical or grammatical errors you notice at the end or in the text of the paper. DO NOT CORRECT THEM. For example, circle misspelled words, but don't write in the correct spelling.

Writers: Read through each editor's comments carefully. Ask questions about anything you don't understand. Remember, it is your paper and you have the option of accepting or rejecting the advice of an editor. When in doubt, ask me—I'm the referee here.

Once you rewrite the first draft based on the peer responses you chose to accept or reject, your teacher will again provide some form of feedback—conferences, workshopping, or electronic draft response. Rewrite your paper a second time based on that response and turn in the third draft for grading.

Process Write for Paper #2

Paper #2 Process Write

Just like the first process write, I want you to write about your writing process for this paper. Listed below are the topics I want you to address (they were given to you for process write #1). In bold are the questions specifically about Paper #2 that I want you to be sure to address. Please write this again not as a list of topics, but rather as a very brief essay—practically a narrative—about how you wrote Paper #2.

1. **In what way/ways did you take Paper #1 and turn it into Paper #2? What did you change? Add? Delete?**
2. **Did the in-class discussion on and practice with reflective writing help you in writing Paper #2?**
3. **What was your goal with Paper #2 and how was that goal different from the goal of Paper #1?**
4. **What did you learn (about yourself, the subject, the world, etc.) from writing this paper?**
5. In writing this paper, what helped you produce the final draft? Was it peer feedback, examples, from the book, me? Did anyone else help you? If so, who was it and how did he/she/they help you?
6. When did you actually write this paper? Did you write it all at once or in parts? Where did you write it? Under what physical circumstances (e.g., standing or sitting, with or without music, with or without food, etc.)?
7. How long did the first draft take? Did the rewrites take less time or more time? Were the re-writes easier or harder to write than the first draft?
8. What do you like best about your paper? Least? Elaborate and show me.
9. What would you do differently if you had the chance to do the paper over and why?

Part Four
The Opinion Paper

ASSIGNMENT THREE: The Opinion Paper

In the first two papers when you moved from personal experience writing to the more complicated analysis of self reflection, you transitioned from writing about a private, individual life event to considering that event within a much broader, more universal context. Now you will follow a similar process in Papers #3 and #4 when you tackle our opinion/argument sequence. In this case you begin with something personal: an issue you wish to learn more about and then support or attack that issue. Your choices involve two distinct but definitely connected assignments that allow you to incorporate into Paper #4 relevant material from Paper #3. The second paper in this sequence also involves researching your topic to provide evidence to support your position on the issue.

Research is always a four-step process involving

1. Locating relevant material,
2. Evaluating that material in terms of its accuracy and authority,
3. Synthesizing that material into a coherent, logical argument or an effective, carefully worked-out solution, and finally
4. Properly documenting and citing all the material you choose to use from the sources you located, evaluated, and worked into your paper.

In this sequence you will first learn to identify and detail your opinion on an issue you care about and then to create a formal researched and documented paper that defends your opinion by successfully completing our mini-research process. The research and organizational skills (synthesizing sources to support logical arguments or explain effective solutions) you learn by writing Papers #3 and #4 will serve you well now in other college courses and later in professional career projects. Everyone has opinions, but, to be an effective human being functioning successfully in our complex society, you need to learn how to explain and support those opinions if you want to be able to convince others to agree with you. And recognizing and solving problems—personal and professional—will always be a part of your day-to-day life in school, at work, or at home. What you learn writing these two assignments will be invaluable for your future success.

*****

Definition of Assignment: Choosing a topic for the opinion paper is the most important step you take in both this assignment and in the next, Paper #4, because, whatever topic you pick, you will be reading and writing about it for the next five or six weeks of the course. So pick something you care about, an issue you have a personal interest in and want to know more about. Writers are, first of all, people with something to say, something that matters to them that they want to communicate to others. In argumentative writing, writers take communication one step further: They want not only to *communicate* their ideas to others but to *convince* those others to agree with them. The opinion paper is the first stage in such argumentative writing; it enables writers to determine *what* they think about a given issue and *why* they think it in the first place. This paper is not a formal argument supported by factual research; that assignment is Paper #4, the mini-research project. Paper #3 is more informal, more loosely structured. In it, you will

- choose and define a controversial issue,
- decide whether you are for or against that issue, and
- give reasons for both your choice of issues and your position on the issue.

Note the word *controversial* before issue. Controversial means in dispute or debatable; a controversial issue is one people disagree about and take sides over. In order for an issue to be controversial, it must have at least two possible positions—usually for and against. What that means for you in Paper #3 is that you must choose a debatable issue, something people argue about, and, if you choose something you care about as well, you probably already have a pro or con position on that issue. When you choose, just remember

1. The issue must be controversial.
2. There must be two or more arguable positions people can take.
3. There must be sources available to support both sides (this is for Paper #4 when you logically argue for your position.)

Prewriting

Freewriting is one of the most effective ways to generate ideas for any writing assignment; it is especially helpful in discovering an issue you might want to write about.

Freewriting prompts for the Opinion Paper:

1. Is there a current issue—international, national or local—that really interests you? Write down everything you know and believe about that issue.
2. Is there something in your world—in family life, school, at work—that you really want to change? Write about the problem and why you feel this way.
3. What do you argue about with your friends, family, or classmates? Do you want to know more about this topic to be able to argue more effectively for it? Describe the topic and your position on it.
4. What do you hate most about _____ and why?

Those are general approaches to discovering a controversial issue. Some specific topics others have chosen in the past might interest you or direct your thinking in a particular area. For example:

- Should athletes who use steroids be allowed to compete professionally?
- Does sexual orientation matter? When? Why?
- Should a university have an attendance policy?
- Is student housing adequate, acceptable, and affordable at WIU?
- How "free" should freedom of expression be? Specifically should hate speech be allowed on a college campus?

Once you have chosen your controversial issue or topic and your position on that topic, you need to generate material for the paper itself; in this specific assignment, you need to explain why you chose your topic and why you take the position you do. Discovering your reasons requires both self-reflection and analysis of the topic itself, both processes you mastered in Paper #2. The following exercises will help you with these processes and familiarize you with the genre you are about to write.

Exercises

#1—Generating Controversial Topics

- Everyone in class freewrites—list as many controversial topics as you can think of.
- Form five groups of four people each. Each group shares all the freewriting lists and synthesizes them into one, eliminating doubles and any noncontroversial topics.
- One member from each group puts their combined list on the board.
- The class goes over each list item by item and decides what is and what is not a controversial topic. The teacher circles each approved topic. The circled items become the approved topics for the class. Other topics must be approved individually by the instructor.

#2—Analyzing Opinion Pieces

Homework assignment from previous class: Find and bring to class a short published opinion piece. It can be an editorial, film review, book review, letter to the editor, or signature column.

- Divide the class into groups.
- Within each group, everyone shares his or her opinion pieces.
- Each group picks one of the pieces to analyze and present to the class. This analysis should include
  1. The topic of the piece and the writer's position on that topic (pro or con),
  2. The writer's reasons for his position, and
  3. The group's opinion on the topic—do they agree or disagree with the writer?
- Each group shares their analysis with the class.

This exercise that you have just completed in group work familiarizes you with both the genesis of opinion pieces and the method of writing them.

#3—For further development of your argument for Paper #3, answer the following questions:

1. What do you already know about your issue?
2. How do you know it?
3. What else do you need to know?
4. How will you go about finding that information?
5. What are the positive qualities of your issue?
6. What are the negative qualities of your issue?
7. Who are your readers?
8. What reasons might you give those readers to persuade them to accept your position?

Opinion readings and other media list:

General possibilities:

- Any current editorial or opinion column on a controversial topic,
- Well written (or maybe even badly written) letters to the editor on controversial topics, and
- Any current TV talk show debate.

A few specific readings:

Anna Quindlen's "Still Needing the F Word"
Kurt Vonnegut's "Cold Turkey" or "Your Guess Is as Good as Mine"
Stephen King's "Why We Crave Horror Movies"
Blaise Cronen's "Burned Any Good Books Lately?"
Hadley Skinner's "In Defense of American Education"
Richard Rodriguez's "Public and Private Language"
Deborah Tanner's "Talking Up Close"
Harvey C. Mansfield's "Grade Inflation: It's Time to Face the Facts"
Linda Lee's "Who Needs College?"

*****

Sample Student Papers
This Masquerade
Landers Duke

Paper III

Legendary African American novelist and Civil Rights activist James Baldwin once said, "The Country's image of the Negro, which hasn't very much to do with the Negro, has never failed to reflect with a kind of terrifying accuracy the state of mind of the country." Baldwin made this comment during a time where Jim Crow laws were at an all time high. I agree with this on an exceedingly deep level. This quote should be taken seriously when closely examining the Negro. If the only outlet to the Negro is through means of entertainment or television as a whole, then the interpreter will already be full of false pretenses.

Americans, including a portion of Blacks, are being poisoned into thinking the Negro is nothing more than a shiftless burden cursed upon this planet we call Earth. Television is the home where most of these stereotypes manifest. People whose only outlet to the Black experience is television are gaining false preconceived notions about Blacks. I agree with Baldwin in the fact that the way the Negro is portrayed upon the mainstream audience is terrifying. If I myself were not a Black man and I watched music videos, played cult video game hits such as GTA San Andreas for hours on end and believed every aspect of the news then I would believe the Negro to be shiftless and docile. Television shows, music videos, movies and even the public news are displaying negative images of Negros and are poisoning the minds of entire races of people.

I feel as though a perfect example would be the black 70s sitcom "Good Times". In the show there are characters such as the black maid, the lazy ignorant buffoon, the angry black man just to name a few. All of these characters perpetuate characters of the minstrel period. Are we as African Americans supposed to accept these behaviors because the cast at large are Blacks? Of course "Good Times" was a box office smash among the White community and even in the Black, but certain stereotypes still hit home with the Black community. All Blacks don't live in the projects. All Blacks don't partake in drinking Kool-Aid. All Blacks don't speak in slang or jive language. Certain aspects of "Good Times" were taken to be facts about all African Americans. Even though most Black television programs resurrect old minstrel shows, most have declined due to the incline of the music video.

As African American children watch music videos, are their minds being trained to think that this is the only way to escape the ghetto? I would have to say yes. I have a theory where the only images available of successful Blacks are on sports cards or in music videos. Music videos and sports are both elements that we as black people have taken as culture. Blacks have taken this as culture because over the centuries, we have gained false values in the fields of vast entertainments. We have embraced them to a point where the country even associates us with the two. Little Black children have been looking up to an admiring gangster rappers and athletes as role models for decades. This has created a ripple effect to a point where we set aside educational values for the fame and fortune of these role models.

This is why the country's image has nothing to do with the Negro. I don't believe the African American culture lies within social entertainment and sports; I believe it lies within our hearts. I am weary of hearing about how Blacks are supreme athletes. For once in my life, I would love to hear how blacks are supreme scholars. We have been forced to believe that we are inferior and are not important if we are not entertaining

continues

Sample Student Papers (*Continued*)
This Masquerade
Landers Duke

the majority. I believe our culture to be that of the African Diaspora, within the language and even everyday customs that we take for granted. If we as a race can grasp our roots, then we as a race can grow at an astronomical rate. Who knows? Maybe even the country's negative image of the Negro could undergo a metamorphosis.

For this metamorphosis to be successful, we must first start at the mainstream level. We must first grasp our children and make them aware that BET is not culture. We must teach them that it's not cool or acceptable to be "gangster," pregnant at 14 years of age or unintelligent but athletic. If we teach these children to value aspects of life such as reading and education then the rest will follow.

I also feel that we must understand our past to understand our future. Blacks such as Baldwin faced several hardships fighting for the rights that some Negros today take for granted. Blacks in the movement were beaten by police officers, hosed by firemen, attacked by dogs and even killed for the rights that are taken for granted today. We as a race cannot even take using a public restroom for granted let alone education. All in all, we must break this masquerade and grow through means of education and we must invest in our youth. For who knows? Your child could be a major partner at a law firm, CEO of a fortune five hundred company, or maybe even president!

Finding the Truth Through the Smoke
Phil Docherty

Paper III

Smoking is a national pastime that I think everyone should take up. It's just as American as baseball and apple pie, if not more so, and the benefits of smoking tobacco greatly outweigh any possible harmful effects. I think you'll find that when you hear the wondrous aspects of this miracle plant, you'll be lighting up fags left and right. Our journey starts in the American colonies in the early 1700s.

Back when our great nation was still considered the New World, tobacco played a great role in society. Not only was it considered medicine, but it was one of our first forms of currency as well. Even our nation's most beloved leader, George Washington, grew 17,000 acres of it until his old ball and chain made him give it up. And everyone was doing it. The pope even rebelled against the church for his inalienable right to light up. How could a man who couldn't tell a lie and a direct relative of God himself, advocate something that is supposedly so harmful to our health? That's right, they couldn't because it isn't.

Smoking tobacco wasn't bad for your health until so called "science" got involved. The Center for Disease Control says that smoking kills 400,000 people a year. This number is a gross overstatement based on an inaccurate computer-generated estimate that doesn't take into account cholesterol, family history, exercise, diet, or even smoking. The real number is closer to 280,000 people a year. Look we just saved the lives of 120,000 people every year who smoke—doesn't that make you feel good? And honestly, what are the chances of you even being in that small group of people at all? It's also a proven fact that cigarette smoking is inescapably intertwined with low Parkinson's and Alzheimer's disease rates.

Not even secondhand smoke is very bad for you. Research has found that children of smokers take ten million more sick days from school than children from non-smoking homes. But I say baloney. Personally, I'd gladly take the risk of possibly getting lung cancer for a three-day weekend. Which brings me to my next point: smoking doesn't cause lung cancer.

Yep, you heard me right; nine out of ten tobacco companies agree that smoking does not cause lung cancer. And whom are you going to believe, a multi-million dollar corporation with researchers, or your high school health teacher who wore those funny looking socks? While it might possibly be true that it **could** cause you to have a higher risk of developing it, smoking does not have an immediate cause-effect correlation like certain "scientists" portray it. It's not like it is with Blue Bunny, where eating ice cream really fast directly causes brain-freeze. And even if there are risks, do you really want to take the risk of getting hit by a bus tomorrow without ever knowing the divine pleasure of God's gift to humanity. Which brings me to another point: if God didn't intend on people drying leaves, wrapping them in paper, burning them, and inhaling that sweet aromatic smoke, then he wouldn't have given us Zippos. And even more so, a life without risk isn't a life worth living.

As I've said before, the benefits of smoking far outweigh the theoretical "risks." The fact of the matter is that cigarettes make you smarter. They calm your nerves and clear your head, allowing you to slow down and take more in. They peacefully subdue your racing mind letting you see things in different ways. I believe that we have tobacco to thank for some of science's greatest discoveries, like $E=MC^2$, seeing as how Einstein was an avid pipe smoker. Did you know that Hitler hated smoking? *Time* magazine reported that, "Adolf Hitler was a fanatical opponent of tobacco." Who would you rather be like?

Evidence for increased intelligence and productivity comes from the fact that smokers work an average of two and one-half hours less each week than their non-smoking coworkers. Then, as a reward for their constant good work, they get smoke breaks, which in turn make them work ever more efficiently. It's a self-perpetuating cycle. Smokers also have better social lives because of their frequent breaks. People become closer to one another over cigarette or pipe. Conversations are started, gossip is shared, and lifelong friendships are forged due solely to this remarkable plant. And lets just face it—smoking makes you look cool and gives you sex appeal. Sure, some people may claim that it makes you "stink" or turns your teeth "yellow," but both of those can be avoided, and isn't that a small price to pay to be one of the coolest and sexiest people in your workplace anyway?

One of the best reasons to start smoking is the rebellion factor. People see you as a kind of James Dean figure with your smoke between your fingers. And nothing quite shows your keen ability to stick it to the man like a lit stogie dangling from your lips. Every time you exhale it says, "I don't care what society thinks or tells me what to do. I'm my own person."

One perk is that people who smoke tend to get the West Nile Virus and other bug related diseases much less frequently because bugs don't like to be around smoke. That's actually one of the big reasons why Native Americans smoked. Another benefit is that you'll never be unprepared to go to a concert—you'll always have a lighter to wave around. Philip Morris, a leading tobacco company, even found a plus side to smoking for the Czech Republic. They published a report that claimed that the country would save about $147 million a year from smokers who wouldn't live long enough to use healthcare or housing for the elderly. It seems that tobacco is the gift that keeps on giving!

continues

Finding the Truth Through the Smoke (*Continued*)
Phil Docherty

And the benefits of smoking are by no means restricted to humans. There is a chimpanzee in China named Ai Ai that took up cigarettes after the death of her mate. She started by taking half smoked butts from tourists and then the zookeepers eventually bought her packs of her own. Years later, she even turned to smoking to help alleviate the pain of losing her daughter to another zoo. If even chimps can appreciate the wonder that is tobacco, isn't it time for you to start?

Writing

Once you have thoroughly familiarized yourself with opinion pieces and have chosen a topic and a position, you are ready to being writing the first draft of Paper #3.

Paper #3: The Opinion Paper

Write a three to five page paper stating, explaining, and supporting your opinion/ position on a controversial issue in today's society. In this assignment you must

- formulate a well constructed, complete thesis,
- defend your position with a sufficient number of reasons clearly stated and explained in detail if necessary, and
- limit your paper to your opinion only, no research necessary.

NOTE: If you do use information from a source, identify that source in the text of your paper. Formal citation is *not* a part of this assignment, but you are still required to identify informally within the text of your paper material from sources.

ALSO: You may address and refute the opposing position near the end of your paper if you wish. Again, this is not a requirement of the opinion paper, but will be an essential inclusion in Paper #4.

Helpful Hints

- Choose a controversial topic that interests you personally. If you are invested in that topic, you will write a better paper.
- Remember your reader, the audience you are trying to convince about the rightness of your position. Think of them as intelligent readers with little or no expertise in your topic.
- Check your tentative working thesis with your teacher and others. Make certain it is complete.
- Write the best possible intro—try to catch your reader's attention right away.
- Hold your reader's interest with clear, coherent and connected reasons for your position.
- Reinforce your conclusion with your reader in mind. Don't just summarize your points.
- Order your points carefully. Start strong and end strong.

*****

We all know that human beings are social but opinionated creatures; almost all of us love to argue, and we're fairly good at it. Our students are no exception. They already know how to argue verbally; they've been arguing with their parents, their siblings, their friends and various authority figures since they learned to talk. But putting their opinions and the reasons for them into writing in an organized, well-developed, easy-to-follow essay is another matter entirely. They need in–class practice dealing with controversial topics to become comfortable with this written form of the argument genre.

Since at this point students have generated enough material to begin drafting their papers out of class, now is a perfect time to use in class time to make them more familiar with argumentative organizational patterns and developmental strategies. Developing a workable complete thesis is the first step in actually writing the paper. Remember, a complete thesis includes both the <u>what</u> and the <u>how</u> of your paper: it identifies your topic and your position on that topic (the <u>what</u>), and it explains how you will go about developing your paper (the <u>how</u>). The following in–class exercise provides practice in developing complete thesis statements.

What Is Your Stance? A Thesis Activity

Each of these 22 questions introduce a different controversial issue, all of which are examples of possible topics for the upcoming opinion paper. In preparation for this paper, it is important to use your critical thinking skills to decide what your stance is on particular issues, and to then turn that stance into a thesis statement.

- After forming a circle with your desks, pass the questions around in a hat, each student drawing one question.
- Read through the question you drew and take a few minutes to consider this issue.
- Decide what your stance/position is in relation to the question.
- Now, on a sheet of paper, rephrase your "answer" into a statement.
- After forming this simple statement, incorporate your reasoning to form a strong thesis statement; do this by looking at your simple statement and asking "Why?"
- Following the circle around the room, each student first reads aloud his/her question to the class and then announces the thesis statement he/she drafted. Students can discuss each other's issues and stances when appropriate, examining the many sides and perspectives to each individual topic.

Example: "Should employers follow affirmative action policies when hiring new employees?"

Step 1, Simple Statement: "Employers should no longer follow affirmative action policies when hiring new employees."

Step 2, Thesis Statement: "Affirmative action policies are a form of reverse discrimination and should no longer be utilized by employers."

Should children be allowed in restaurants?
Is everyone in the US entitled to affordable health care?
Should antidepressants be prescribed through any doctor? How easy should it be to receive a prescription?

continues

What Is Your Stance? A Thesis Activity (*Continued*)
Should college athletes be paid?
Should prison inmates be offered schooling to earn degrees?
Should safe haven laws be enforced? (Safe haven laws allow mothers to abandon their babies at local fire stations and other "drop off" places)
Should a state's residents be given priority for job openings in that state?
Should English be the official language of the US?
Should paparazzi be allowed in the United States?
Should casinos reject business from gambling addicts?
Should child actors' money be accessible to their parents?
Should athletes who test positive for drug use be considered for the Hall of Fame?
Should working mothers receive more paid emergency days than their coworkers?
Does hip-hop and other rap music have a positive or negative influence on society?
Should child predators be granted parole?
Since it is classified as a type of amputation, should it be legal to have a cat declawed?
Should college athletes be required to maintain a certain GPA to continue playing sports?
Should adoptive parents be required to tell their adopted children who their biological parents are?
Should high school aged adolescents receive doctor-patient confidentiality, thus keeping important information from their parents? (For example, abortions, suicide attempts, cutting, etc.)
Should priests report serious crimes they find out about during confessions?
At a certain age, should senior citizens' drivers licenses be taken away or reconsidered?
Should employers be required to hire a certain number of employees with disabilities (mental or physical)?

When developing a complete thesis, a writer should remember that, in opinion/argument papers, that thesis needs to be a strong one as well. A <u>strong</u> thesis asserts a <u>position</u> that

- Requires careful analysis to support and develop it.
- Provides a point about your particular case that would not be immediately obvious to readers.

Conversely, a <u>weak</u> thesis

- Makes no real claims or asserts no real position ("This paper looks at the pros and cons of gun control laws.").
- Makes an obviously true claim or is just a statement of fact ("Obesity is unhealthy.").
- Restates well-known, accepted clichés. ("Love is blind.").
- States an overly broad, unprovable generalization ("Cooperation is always necessary").

While writers often alter or even reverse their initial positions as they reshape their papers and/or discover new reasons or evidence for their position, at any given point in time writers always need a working <u>tentative</u> thesis (tentative because it is not set in concrete but is rather fluid and can therefore be altered to fit new evidence or accommodate a shifting position) because it serves as a road map for the paper they are writing. That tentative thesis should always

- be one that can be managed within the parameters of time (days before due date) and space (length of paper),
- asserts something specific, and
- delineates a specific position, plan for action, etc.

During prewriting you discovered a series of reasons for the stance that you chose on your controversial topic. Now that you have formulated a workable thesis, you must focus on developing those reasons into the body of your paper in a coherent, readable pattern. Practicing this kind of focus and development with your peers enables you to better organize and flesh out your own paper as you write it.

Developing Controversial Topics

- Divide the class into pairs and have each pair pick a topic from the controversial hat. If the pair is dissatisfied with their choice, they may return the topic and pick <u>once</u> more only.
- Once the topic is chosen, within each pair, students decide who is for and who is against the topic.
- Allow the pairs a short period of time, five to eight minutes tops, to write down a list of reasons for their positions.
- Each pair in turn then presents these positions and the reasons for them to the class.
- As the audience to be convinced, after each for and against presentation, the class chooses a winner.

If more practice is needed, have each pair switch sides and argue the opposite position.

Informal Debate Exercise

To help you and your classmates get used to argument and counterargument, complete this group exercise in class.

Divide into four groups of approximately five each. On a first come, first serve basis, each group should pick one of the following argumentative issues (or have the groups draw one of the four from a hat):

1. It should be mandatory for all college students to participate in a volunteer service activity.
2. Cell phones should not be allowed in restaurants.
3. Women should be allowed to play in male professional sports leagues when there is no female equivalent.
4. Hate groups such as the KKK or the Nazi's should not be allowed to demonstrate or disperse literature on college campuses.

Each member of the group should consider his/her position on the issue and write down his/her thoughts, listing as many reasons as he/she can for the position chosen. Then, in group discussion, each should offer his/her viewpoint to try to persuade the rest of the group to agree with that viewpoint. The aim of each group is to come to consensus on one side or the other of the issue they are discussing.

When each group has determined a position on their issue, they will list the reasons for their position and present those to the class.

Controversial Hot Topics List:

1. Prior to entering college, should high school graduates be required to complete one year of volunteer/community service? Defend your position.
2. Should non-natural born US citizens be allowed to run for, and possibly become, President of the United States? Defend your position.
3. Should celebrities be allowed a "zone of privacy" where paparazzi are not allowed? Defend your position.
4. Recently, models with a low Body Mass Index (BMI) have been banned from fashion shows. Do you agree with this? Defend your position.
5. Should fine arts programs (art, music, theater) receive the same funding as athletic programs? Defend your position.
6. Should English be the official language of the United States? Defend your position.
7. Should restaurants ban cell phone use? Defend your position.
8. Should schools be segregated by gender? Defend your position.
9. Should there be laws requiring young girls to get the HPV vaccine? Defend your position.
10. Should registered sex offenders have their parental rights taken away? Defend your position.
11. Should women be included in the draft if it is ever reinstated? Defend your position.
12. Should same sex couples be able to adopt children? Defend your position.
13. Should schools require all students to be fluent in a second language? Defend your position.
14. Should public schools be able to distribute contraceptives to students without parental permission? Defend your position.
15. Should "unhealthy alternatives" (i.e., pop, candy, etc.) be allowed in school cafeterias? Defend your position.
16. Should the government have a say in who can have children? Defend your position.
17. Should HIV/AIDS tests be available over the counter like a pregnancy test? Defend your position.
18. Should cell phone use be banned when operating a motor vehicle? Defend your position.
19. Should Supreme Court justices have restricted terms instead of the current lifetime appointments? Defend your position.
20. Should the Electoral College be dissolved and presidents directly elected? Defend your position.
21. Should freshmen and sophomores be required to live on campus?
22. Should there be enforced caps on the price of college textbooks?

A third possible activity during the writing stage is returning to one of the texts from the reading section (or choosing a new one entirely) and analyzing it rhetorically to extract its organizational structure and rhetorical strategies. This extraction can provide students with more alternatives for developing and organizing their own papers.

Rewriting

The revision units at the end of Part III are equally applicable for revision in Papers #3, #4, and #6. You should revise your opinion papers based on peer and teacher feedback concerning the effectiveness of your written piece in persuading your readers.

Peer Response for Paper #3, the Opinion Paper

1. List two problems you want peers to help you with.
2. What is especially interesting or effective in this draft? After reading it, what do you remember about it?
3. What are the author's topic and position on that topic?
4. Comment on the opening paragraph. Does it address the audience? Give suggestions for improvement.
5. Number the reasons the writer gives for his position. Are they sufficient? Do any need further explanation or detail? Identify those and make suggestions for improvement.
6. Is the conclusion complete? Strong? Could it be improved? Make specific suggestions.
7. Is the paper well organized? Should any paragraph be moved to another part of the paper? Identify it and suggest where it should be placed.
8. Suggest parts of this draft that could be cut from the next draft and explain why those parts are unnecessary
9. Is the argument convincing? Did it convince you? Point to the parts that you found most convincing. Or, if you aren't convinced, what would the writer need to add to convince you?

After peer response, you should rewrite, consulting the instructor in class and/or during office hours about what to shift, add, delete, or alter.

*****

Self-reflection remains key to writing improvement. Therefore, we continue to require students to write thoughtful, complete process papers after completing an assignment.

Process Paper for Paper #3, the Opinion Paper

1. Why did you choose this topic?
2. In what ways, if any, has your opinion changed or developed during the writing of this paper?
3. What did you want to accomplish with this paper *or* what was your purpose in writing it (other than that it was required)? Do you feel you accomplished that purpose?
4. Please reflect on your supporting reasons for your position. Do you think you have sufficient support? Did you include counterpoints? Do you think they helped support your thesis? Please explain.
5. In writing this paper, what helped you produce the final draft? Was the peer feedback helpful? Were the in-class discussions helpful? Did the examples from the book help? Did anyone else help you? If so, who was it and how did he/she/they help you?
6. Do you feel the exercises on generating a thesis statement were helpful in any way? Please explain your answer.
7. Do you feel the small group exercises on generating support and organizing your paper were helpful in any way? Please explain your answer.
8. Please describe your actual writing process. Include the physical circumstances and what you went through in writing this paper.
9. What do you like best about your paper? Least? Please be specific and explain.
10. What would you do differently if you had the chance to do the paper over? Why?

Part Five
The Mini-Research Position Paper

ASSIGNMENT FOUR: The Mini-Research Position Paper

In writing Paper #2, you learned to truly revise, or (re)vision a subject—your personal narrative—and rework the same material into an entirely different paper, the reflection essay. During that process you internalized, perhaps without realizing it, the basic principles of Macro Revision discussed near the end of the preceding section. Now you will put into play those principles as you (re)vision your opinion paper and turn it into a formal researched and documented argument.

Actually, this (re)vision is much easier than it appears on the surface. As a writer you already have

- your topic—the controversial issue you chose for Paper #3,
- your position on that topic, and
- your reasons for that position

and possibly, if you feel that it was effective in Paper #3, the structure (organization) of Paper #4 as well.

Now you need to add evidence from sources to your argument by mastering the three steps of research:

I. **Locating effective evidence through secondary and/or primary research**
II. **Evaluating those sources for their**
   A. **validity of material**
   B. **authenticity of source**
   C. **relevance to your argument**
III. **Integrating that evidence smoothly into the right places in your own paper with**
   A. **direct quotations properly cited (for a paper the length of this one, long quoted passages seldom work—there's too much of another person's writing in your paper; short or partial quotes worked into your own sentences prove most effective in this kind of assignment)**
   B. **paraphrases, also properly cited (putting someone else's writing into your own words and then referencing the source as you did with a direct quote)**

C. **Brief summaries of sources, again properly cited (the summary skills you learned at the beginning of Paper #2 come in handy here)**
D. **valid data, properly cited (statistics, names, dates, places, case studies, narrative examples, etc.)**

Unlike Paper #3, in this assignment, every reason for your opinion must be *proven* with relevant evidence from a reliable source.

Example, "Most students at Western prefer to live in dorms rather than off campus." Perhaps most people you know do feel that way. But how many of the 11,000 plus Western students do you know personally? Maybe a few dozen? What about the other 10,950? In other words, you believe your assertion to be true, but to convince others, you must *prove* your assertion. How would you go about that?

Well, first you could research back issues of *The Courier* to see if articles on student living preferences exist. Next, you could ignore the word "Western" for a moment and check into other campus newspapers and websites to see if they support your position. Both these are *secondary* sources because you are locating and using other people's research to support your own.

But, in this case, you could also do *primary* research on your own; that is, design and conduct a survey sampling the opinion of X number of Western students. You might even choose a certain number of Freshmen, Sophomores, Juniors and Seniors to see if their preferences change as they progress through college.

Now, what if your survey invalidates (contradicts) your original assertion? What if Western students prefer living off campus? Can you still write your paper? Actually you can, if you reverse your position and alter your thesis accordingly. You are arguing the same issue from the other side.

IV. **Documenting your evidence by correctly citing each source—quotes, para-phrases, summaries, etc.—and listing those sources in proper format on your works cited page. Because formats for parenthetical citation and works cited pages are covered in your manual, this text concerns itself only with what to cite, how often to cite, and where to place the citation in your text.**

*****

Prewriting

As you begin (re)visioning or converting the opinion paper into the research paper, you need to envision this project as a step-by-step project. Your work in this project extends over the next four to five weeks of class, so it is important to focus on the individual but related tasks as they arise, to complete each on time, and move on to the next. In this assignment your understanding the research process is actually as important as the paper you produce in the end. To ensure that you master that process, so essential for college level work, we include here a chronological checklist for accomplishing the mini research project. Each stage on this list must be successfully completed before you begin the next.

Checklist:

1. Reread Paper #3 and decide if you wish to retain
   - its stance
   - its organization
   - any other parts—the intro, a particularly good passage, etc.

If you do choose to retain these three, go on to item #2 on the checklist. If you wish to change all or any of these three, use the following "What's the Question" exercise to refocus and perhaps even reorganize your material before you begin Paper #4.

What's Your Question?

First take out a blank sheet of paper and, using an easy-to-read marker, write down four things:

1. Your tentative thesis statement
2. The reason you chose your topic
3. A list of what you already know about your topic
4. A list of what you still want to know about it

Hang your paper on the classroom wall and go around the class and read everyone else's paper. On each paper, add a question about what else you would like to know about that topic. After you have completed reading and suggesting for everyone else's paper, go back to your own. You should now have a considerably longer list of things to check out about your own topic. Take the list home and let it help you decide what you need to research in this assignment.

---

2. List your points that need evidence to support them and begin locating those sources.
3. Attend library research orientation.
4. Locate and bring to class three or more sources required for this paper.
5. Evaluate those sources and choose those you need.
6. If you have enough sources to cover all your points and meet the assignment's requirements, you are ready to organize your paper. Follow the organization you chose for Paper #3 or the new order you created after determining that Paper #3 was flawed.
   Organize your material in the order you chose. Fill out the chart provided in this chapter for this organization.
7. Write a first draft using that chart for ordering materials and using sources.
8. Integrate the source material under the relevant points, making sure to cite all direct quotes, paraphrases, and any specific data (statistics, dates, percentages, examples, etc.) you incorporated from sources.
9. Submit that draft for a group conference (peer and teacher) response or for peer and teacher response separately in that order.
10. Redraft with responder suggestions in mind. Again, make sure <u>all</u> source material is documented.
11. Using the citations, create a formal <u>Works Cited</u> list for the paper.
12. Submit this draft for brief feedback in class.
13. Rewrite one more time to deal with any problems that surfaced in the second round of response (perhaps a peer editing, possibly teacher commentary in class).
14. Proofread, clean up surface errors, check citation and documentation formats, and turn in paper.

*****

The first step in completing Paper #4 is collecting supportive evidence for your position by (1) developing relevant primary sources and (2) locating valid, usable secondary ones.

Developing and Using Primary Sources

There are several basic instruments of primary research: surveys, interviews, and observations. Because the results of these instruments are unpredictable in advance (you don't know what the students think about housing until you ask them) and can sometimes contradict your original position, it is best to conduct primary research first. If you locate secondary material before conducting primary research, you may have to scrap many of those original sources if you change your position on the issue. So, to avoid two secondary source search processes, complete and assess your primary sources first.

Primary research matters for a number of reasons. First, it focuses specifically on your research needs. Survey questions, interview formats, and observation criteria are designed *by* you *for* your particular investigation. Second, conducting this research just before you write your paper ensures that you have up-to-date information for evidence. And third, you can uncover unexpected and significant information directly relating to your topic.

For best results, primary research requires focus. Survey and interview questions should be as specific as possible.

- Target what you need to know.
- Phrase questions clearly and directly.
- Design the primary research implement (whether a survey, interview, or observation) impartially—don't let your bias show.
- Tabulate, analyze, and report your results fairly.

Surveys and Questionnaires

Usually in the form of a series of questions or statements, this instrument can help you determine what a given group of people think about your controversial issue. In some cases, it can also reveal why that particular group thinks the way it does.

Helpful Hints: What NOT To Do

1. Do NOT ask two questions in the same sentence.
2. Do NOT include vague or ambiguous questions.
3. Avoid slanted questions.

If questions require choices, develop checklists to facilitate ease for your responders. The easier the survey is to complete, the more responses you are likely to get back. Before you conduct your survey,

- Test it on a sample group to ensure clarity and usability.
- Select your actual group carefully. Make sure it's large enough to yield a valid result. Choose a group that is likely to know about and have a stake in your issue.

When you finish, tabulate the results and incorporate them into your paper.

NOTE: When you begin that incorporation, make certain to include a brief description of your survey—its purpose, scope, and results—so that readers understand that this survey will be one source of your evidence.

Interviews

Interviews are an accessible and valuable method of obtaining information and opinions from others. Like surveys, their success depends on (1) careful selection of the interviewee, (2) thorough preparation by the interviewer, and (3) professional conducting of the interview itself.

1. Choosing the interviewee: Whom you choose is determined by what you want to know. You may need an expert or authority to validate a point or an ordinary person directly involved in and affected by your issue to provide a sense of reality and immediacy.

2. Thorough preparation: Do your homework. Learn as much as you can about your interviewee and the area of expertise in question. Then develop and write out a list of key questions in advance. Remember that good questions allow for elaboration and detail. When preparing your list, remember that the number of questions depends on the time frame of the interview. Arrange your questions in order of importance, with the most important first, in case you run out of time.

3. Conducting the interview: Arrive a little early to get your bearings. Bring a notepad and pen, or if you have received permission in advance, bring your tape recorder. Allow a few minutes of small talk for "warming up" before you plunge into the "meat" of the interview. Don't try to write down every word—a phrase or two for an idea will suffice. If you want an exact quote, ask the interviewee to go slowly and write down the remark precisely. Always thank the person for granting the interview and offer to send a copy of the final paper or finished report as a professional courtesy. Go home and write up the details of the interview while they are still fresh in your mind.

Observations

Personal direct observation remains one of the most effective ways of obtaining evidence for argumentative theses. For example, if you want to determine the level of violence in children's programming, watch as many of those programs as possible carefully for a period of time. Or if you wish to discover how many students use Starbucks at Western's Student Union daily, sit outside and count the customers from 8 A.M. to 3 P.M. In either case, direct observation is the simplest, and often the quickest, way to gather the information you need.

To observe any situation effectively, you must first decide on the purpose of your observation because the purpose determines what you will observe in the first place. Then choose the best possible site for your observation—if you are trying to find out who shops at Wal-Mart, station yourself at the front entrance. Don't trust your memory; take careful notes or videotape or photographs during the observation. Be sure to note the time and place and the background, the scene itself, to put the observation into context. For accuracy, record *only* what you see, *not* what you think or expect to see.

Your final report can take several forms:

- a narrative over a period of time
- a description of what you observed
- a process record when what you are observing occurs in stages (an assembly line building a car)
- a cause and effect analysis if you are reporting what happens as a result of a certain occurrence (testing a tornado siren in a mall, for example)

In observation, as in interviewing and surveying, you are the researcher discovering the evidence you will then use to support your case. There is no middleman recording data for you to locate, no sociologist who analyzed crime statistics and recorded them, no doctor reporting on a new drug discovery for AIDS. Primary research can be innovative and original and exciting, and it provides a real balance against the dusty library shelves and endlessly linked internet sites.

*****

Locating and Evaluating Secondary Sources

Once upon a time. . . .

Locating and evaluating secondary sources is the better known and more familiar research process. This research involves using library resources like books, journals, newspapers, magazines, government documents, etc. In the past students conducted this research in their campus libraries by methodically checking through card catalogues and periodical and newspaper indexes to locate books and articles related to their topic. After physically locating the texts themselves, they photocopied relevant pages from non-circulating journals and actually checked out relevant books. Next they read through those sources and evaluated them for

- accuracy or validity,
- authority, and
- relevance to their topic.

Once you had chosen your sources, you went through them carefully, taking notes, highlighting, and perhaps even color-coding to identify what source material related to particular parts in your paper. Finally you organized your notes and started to draft your paper.

But, in the Information Age. . . .

Today most of the library work can be done on the computer, a technological device our students have no problem operating. Indeed, computer literacy now begins in kindergarten. Instead of card catalogues and indexes, today's researchers use search engines, each designed to cover specific fields or kinds of publications. At WIU, and most colleges and universities, search engines can be found on the institution's library home page. Specific lists of available information can be located by typing in specific <u>keywords</u> that identify, as narrowly as possible, the topic being researched.

> For example, if you are researching a particular author, just typing in the name will not narrow the list sufficiently. Say you are researching the roles of women in Shakespeare's plays. Typing in <u>William Shakespeare</u> only will illicit 50,000 or more references. Typing in <u>Shakespeare's plays</u> will reduce the list only slightly. Typing <u>women in Shakespeare's plays</u> will narrow the list significantly. If you are only dealing with one type of Shakespeare play, say the comedies, replacing the last word, "plays," with "comedies" will narrow the list even further. And if you are only focusing on two or three plays, adding their titles will give you a very workable list.

Remember that the Internet also provides excellent websites under URL addresses—the Library of Congress, all US federal agencies, and NOVA links are just three examples. Students should remember to bookmark useful sites to reduce time locating them again for additional research.

At the request of the course instructor the WIU Library conducts introductory research classes for the required writing courses and any other classes involving research. Additionally, individual instructors often supplement the library session with in-class research exercises whenever computer labs are available.

For example, here are some Google search tips to get you started:

Using Google

Google is another fast and often accurate search engine when you are locating information for your paper on the internet:

Finding reliable sources can be tricky, but there are a few Google tips that can save you the headache of sifting through endless pages of information that your teacher won't let you use because the web sites are not considered reliable. Refining your searches to look only at pages that end in "gov," "edu," or "org" is a good way to get reliable data for your papers. To set these limits, simply add site:gov, site:edu or site:org to your search box. This limiting will return only searches that provide information from government agencies, educational institutions, or organizations. However, you still need to check that the individual resource material you locate this way is reliable. Using the limiting technique does cut back on pulling up blogs and biased/fictitious material, but it doesn't cut it out completely.

Another way to search the internet for reliable information is to use Google Scholar, a specific search engine that can be found at http://scholar.google.com.

This engine, just like the university library databases, provides search results from academic journals and books that are usually very reliable. Happy searching.

Evaluating Sources

Of course, sources located electronically still undergo the same evaluative processing applied to traditional library sources. Is the material reliable? Is the authority authentic? Is the information provided relevant to your argument? Not all sources, especially those located on the Internet, are reliable. Anyone can establish a web site and put anything on that web site. Student researchers need to be particularly cautious about accepting internet sources at face value. There are questions you can ask about an Internet source to evaluate its reliability:

- Is the web address a *.com* or a *.org*? Most educational institutions are .edu, federal government sites are .gov, and libraries .edu, .gov, or .com, depending on their affiliation, and therefore more reliable.
- What credentials do the web site authors have that make them authorities on the issue you are researching? For example, a doctor is an expert on medical questions; a chemist or a biologist can explain toxic effects on the environment; or a professor of history can detail a Civil War battle.
- What evidence do the authors use to prove their points or support their position? Is that evidence reliable? Sufficient? For instance, if you found a source using an opinion poll, was that poll objective or slanted? How many people were polled? Was the sample large enough? Who was polled? Was it a sufficient cross section of the population?
- When was this information published on the website? Is it too old to be useful?
- Only the researcher/writer can answer this last question: Is the information useful for my paper?

The same kinds of questions apply to published material:

- What are the author's credentials?
- Who (what publishing house) published the book or article and when?
- Is the piece slanted or objective?
- Is the evidence solid? Was it obtained through objective, in-depth research?
- Is it relevant to your project?

Practice in evaluating sources will help you judge your own data. On the next page is a research scenario to help you learn to evaluate sources.

Evaluating Sources Exercise

Name: _____

     For your research paper in another course, your teacher has assigned you the topic of AIDS in Botswana, Africa. You have been asked to find the most reliable and helpful source available using the internet. Since your English 180 instructor is such a nice person, she has already searched the internet and found four sources discussing your topic for you. It is now your job to evaluate these four sources to see which will be the best one for you to use in your other class.

     Using the questions listed previously in this text, evaluate the usefulness and accuracy of each article below.

Avert Organization
http://www.avert.org/aidsbotswana.htm
___ Useful/Reliable ___ Unreliable/not useful
Why:

The Onion
http://www.theonion.com/content/node/40976/print/
___ Useful/Reliable ___ Unreliable/not useful
Why:

The New York Times
http://query.nytimes.com/gst/fullpage.html?sec=health&res=9D05E0DF153AF935A2 5754C0A9629C8B63
You can search for this title: "Devastated by AIDS, Africa Sees Life Expectancy Plunge" by Celia. W. Dugger
___ Useful/Reliable ___ Unreliable/not useful
Why:

Academic Search Premier
For this last article, you should go to the WIU library homepage. You will need to click on Select a Database. Then choose Academic Search Premier. Then search for this title: "Gender and HIV/AIDS in Botswana: A Focus on Inequalities and Discrimination" in *Gender and Development*.
___ Useful/Reliable ___ Unreliable/not useful
Why:

The best way to record the results of your evaluation of sources is to create an annotated bibliography. Although not required by every instructor, the annotated bibliography proves that you completed the evaluation process and located enough relevant sources for your paper while it also provides you with an instantly available checklist for locating the source of a specific piece of information. For example, where were those percentages about violent crime rising? Look at the bibliography to see what source dealt with those statistics instead of rifling through notes from several sources before you find the right one. Additionally, creating the annotated bibliography gives students practice in the works cited formats they will need for their final draft.

The Annotated Bibliography

For Paper #4, the research paper, you are required to have a minimum of three credible sources. (Remember, wikipedia.org is **not** a credible source. If you find 'good' information on that site, corroborate it with another source.) You are to provide copies of each of your sources. If you use a book, magazine, newspaper, etc. for a source, you need to photocopy the original source and include the photocopy in your folder.

In addition to the photocopies, you must include an annotated bibliography. Annotated bibliographies provide the reader with publication information—the "works cited" information—as well as a summary of each text you used. Please refer to the Hacker manual (p. 113-152) for information on creating a works cited entry. There is not an example in that book of an annotation, so I will provide some guidelines and examples for you to follow from an article on the web about annotations. When formatting the annotated bibliography, model it after the MLA style works cited page, which is exemplified on page 152. Substitute "Annotated Bibliography" where it says "Works Cited." (Leave out the quotation marks, of course.) Remember to include your last name in the top right header along with the appropriate page number.

The following information (except the final annotation) comes from St. Cloud University's website. (http://leo.stcloudstate.edu/acadwrite/annotated.html#Longer)

Guidelines for creating an annotated bibliography

1. List the completed bibliographical citation.
2. Explain the main purpose of the work.
3. Briefly describe the content.
4. Indicate the possible audience for the work.
5. Evaluate the relevance of the information.
6. Note any special features.
7. Warn readers of any defect, weakness, or bias.

These annotations should be concise but thorough.

Annotation Examples

Only the first entry has been double-spaced to save space on the handout. Please double space each entry like the first one here. Do not include extra spaces between entries. Do not include a space between the entry and the annotation.

For a newspaper article—

Dembart, Lee. "Fears on DNA Studies Fade, but Won't Die," <u>Los Angeles Times</u>, April 12,

1980, Part I, p. 1ff.

Dembart claims that fears of "Andromeda Strain" are unfounded. An interesting quote by James D. Watson, co-discoverer of DNA, asserts his scientific opinion about the genetic controversy: "I think the whole thing is lunacy. . . . I helped raise these issues, but within six months I was acutely embarrassed. There's no evidence that anyone has gotten sick from any of this" (3). On a more speculative note, Dembart quotes Robert Sinsheimer, who acknowledges fears are less justified than originally thought, but also suspects that genetic engineering could conceivably result in a new route for the transmission of cancer (5). This article seems to provide a fairly balanced, up-to-date overview of the whole issue.

For a book—

Howard, Ted, and Jeremy Rifkin. <u>Who Should Play God?</u> New York: Dell 1977.

This book "lifts the cloak of secrecy from genetic experiments" and explores, among other things, "who is performing the research and who profits from it" (12). It's clearly anti-genetic engineering; its chapter titles give a good idea of the direction and flavor of the book, for example, "Eugenics," "Eliminating 'Bad' Genes," "Bio-Futures," "Scientists and Corporation." This book looks as if it is an appropriate source for the social arguments from the political left wing.

For a personal interview—

Potter, Kelly. Personal interview. 25 Mar. 2007.

Miss Potter, a graduate assistant at Western Illinois University spoke very positively about her experiences teaching English 180. She feels that teaching four sections of freshman composition gives graduate students the opportunity to gain classroom experience necessary for a competitive job market. This interview was conducted in person at Miss Potter's office.

Readings

Instructors can use any researched and documented article from an online scholarly journal that can be downloaded by students and used for in class discussions. The focus of this textual examination is to discover how professional writers (in this case probably English professors simply because freshman composition uses MLA documentation formats)

- Introduce research activities
- Prove specific points

- Integrate evidence from sources into their own text
- Handle short quotes and paraphrases
- Cite sources parenthetically (<u>what</u> they cite and <u>how</u> they cite it)
- Create a works cited list for the paper (what goes in it, where each item goes, and how the items and the list are formatted and punctuated)

Rather than lecture on (tell) the important research tasks, we choose to illustrate (show) how experienced writers accomplish them. Taking students through a sample paper and highlighting these seven tasks helps them *see* how, step by step, this research and writing process can be accomplished. To reinforce the professional sample, we include here a sample student text as well. Others are available in the Writing Program annual publication of *Western Voices*, the collection of prize winning student essays from last year's writing classes.

For many kids and young teenagers, school is just part of the everyday routine. For the kids that are part of the routine, they learn discipline and the consequences of good and bad behavior, along with the feeling of accomplishment from a good grade. All these factors play an important role in the development for children that can lead to a positive future in society. Unfortunately, there are many children across the nation who come from poverty-stricken neighborhoods with inadequate education systems. The sad truth is that many of these children will one day join, according to the Bureau of Justice Statistics, the 750,000 inmates who currently populate our prisons nationwide (U.S. Dept of Justice). One way to address this problem is in early prevention for these children. Unfortunately, there is a current problem in the overwhelming numbers of inmates already populating our prison system that needs to be addressed. The most efficient and effective way to address this problem is to improve the support of educational programs offered to inmates. This will not only improve their chances of being a successful citizen upon release, but can better our society as a whole.

The pressures of living in a poverty-stricken environment can overwhelm even the brightest and smartest of people. With the minimum wage currently set at $6.50 (Dennis Cauchon), many are stuck supporting a family on this rate and find themselves barely making ends meet. What increases the feeling of stress is when the reason they find themselves trapped in this situation is due to their lack of education.

These stresses can lead even an intelligent person to a bad decision in times of desperation. The truth is that, despite our preconceived notions that all criminals are murderers, the Bureau of Justice Statistics states that over 60% of inmates are currently serving time for non-violent drug related crimes (U.S. Dept of Justice). These convictions, however, don't automatically justify labeling all inmates as cruel and unchangeable criminals. There are many reasons behind these crimes that often go unnoticed. For example, stated by the special report done by U.S. Dept. of Justice Office, of the total inmates entering the state prisons, 54% don't have a high school diploma. the poverty level of these inmates should not be an excuse for their wrong choices, yet, the extenuating circumstances leading illiterate and poverty-stricken citizens to prison cannot be ignored.

Although time spent in prison is meant to be a punishment, it can also offer a good opportunity for inmates to grow intellectually. Sometimes the reason behind the criminal acts these individuals commit is that the act was just another part in the negative cycle they encounter on the streets. Once in prison, and the pressures of their negative environment alleviated, an inmate can actually give focus to something more positive.

continues

The advantages of educational programs offered to inmates will benefit the inmate's future after prison by breaking the destructive pattern they were once in on the streets. These educational programs are capable of strengthening their knowledge and self worth. Simply enriching an inmate's self-esteem can give them the drive they need to change their lives for the better.

In a study done by Sandy Cutshall, the state of Virginia is one of the few states taking educational programs seriously, and has adopted the theme, "fighting crime through education." The state has a specific branch, The Department of Correctional Education (DCE), which rests all its focus on the adult and youth correctional facilities throughout the entire state. The Department has a staff of over 750 teachers that function as their own school district. They provide opportunities for inmates to attend classes to graduate from high school, receive their GED, and complete functional literacy classes. The inmates are even offered opportunities to be certified in a vocational trade like carpentry and electrical work upon release. The effort that the state of Virginia is giving to the inmates is not going unnoticed. Inmates are able to discover a talent or a skill that can be applied to a job, which is giving them a new hope to better job placements and over all better self-esteem. (Cutshall)

One of the many teachers that Cutshall studied in the Virginia prison education system is Bonnie Cutwright, a optical technology course instructor for the Fluvanna Correctional Center for Women in Troy, Virginia. Cutwright is able to see firsthand the positive changes in inmates, "It is tremendous to see the change in self-esteem these women can experience when they learn new skills." (Cutshall) Despite the common stigma tagged to the safety of a teacher in a prison environment, Cutwright has learned otherwise from her students.

For many, the view of a classroom full of women or men all dressed alike completing one of many checks of every item they are using may seem intimidating to some, but Cutwright chooses to look past the misleading exteriors and tries to enhance the good within the women.

Bonnie is not the only teacher in Cutshall's study who gives faith to the inmates, Randy Estes does as well. Estes teaches carpentry at Indian Creek Correctional Center in Chesapeake, Virginia. His facility mainly deals with the substance abuse in the community and is one of the largest in the nation. Like Cutwright, Estes is able to witness the thirst an inmate has to learn. Estes states, "It is a point of pride when they have mastered something new and it goes up on the board" (Cutshall) Estes also credits this enlightenment with the overall good behavior displayed by the student inmates. In fact, according to Estes, in his overall experiences the attitude and behaviors are more positive in his students than in those outside the program (Cutshall).

A problem these programs are facing is the skepticism of our society that criminals don't deserve a free education. However, the effort in setting up and maintaining educational programs in prison does not only give benefit to the inmates alone. These programs have ways of benefiting our society as a whole.

One of the many positive things America is known for is the availability of jobs. Currently the prison industry employees over 500,000 people, which, under General Motors, is our countries leading employer. (Bureau of Justice Statistics) Looking at the prison education system in Virginia, they have developed their own school district, which resembles the school districts that teach our nation's children. In both cases, teachers are needed to lead the classrooms, administrators needed to address academic policies and most importantly, in both cases there are students eager to learn.

A more practical angle to these educational programs is the completion of tasks by inmates in their learning process. For example, inmates in glass making classes can provide dishware for the cafeterias, those interested in the culinary arts prepare food in the kitchens, and custodial maintenance services are provided throughout the prison. The outcome of these services during the 1999-2000 fiscal year for the DCE in Virginia generated a live work savings of around $880,000. (Cutshall)

The tasks being completed by the inmates in their course studies are also reaching out to the surrounding community. In order to complete many of the vocational certificates the inmates are aiming for, they are required to complete high-quality projects. A good example of this is displayed at the craft shows in the community, Woodworks in particular. Woodworks is a craft show displaying the works of the inmates that are put up for sale. According to Cutshall, DCE found that, most recently, this activity raised $13,000, which was distributed throughout the community. Some of Estes' students had projects displayed and earned $1,600 of the total.

Unfortunately, as many tax paying citizens like to point out, the support of these programs will cause an overall tax increase across the nation. In addressing this concern, tax payers need to look at the bigger picture that can be obtained from these programs. According to the DCE in Cutshall's study, "over half the offenders released from institutions each year will return within three years." The numbers are larger for those left uneducated than those of the educated inmates. Overcrowding is a well known problem facing the prison system today. Taxpayers are supporting the expanding and building of new prisons each year. Educating our inmates while they spend their time in jail can help reduce the number of returning inmates each year, which will in turn lessen the amount of taxes we need to pay.

Not only is the return rate affected by these education programs, but the educated inmates being released can finally be given an opportunity to be employed at a decent paying job. The benefit of better job placements doesn't just affect inmates alone, but the tax payers as well. When considering the tax increases that are caused by the education programs, the released inmates themselves are given the chance to give back to the programs. In having a better paying job, they are able to directly contribute to the taxes and can join the rest of the tax paying citizens. Obtaining a job can benefit the overall cause of educational programs in so many ways.

When considering all the advantages and disadvantages of educating our prison inmates, it is clear to see that the advantages weigh heavier for support of educational programs. Despite all our preconceived notions that all these men and women are cold blooded and have no hope, all it takes is someone to offer them a second chance. Simply educating inmates can do so much for not only their futures, but the overall future of our country. Providing a better future after release and supporting the employment force for our nation are just a few of the things that can go on the list of benefits for the education of our prisoners. However, there are many more benefits in educating our prisoners, in which our society needs to realizes can make our country a better place to live.

Works Cited

Cauchon, Dennis. "States Say $5.15 an Hour Too Little." <u>USA Today</u> 30 May 2005. 01 Nov. 2006.

Cutshall, Sandy. "Teaching Hope Behind Bars." (2001): 22. <u>Expanded Academic ASAP</u>. 09 Oct. 2006.

U.S. Department of Justice. Bureau of Justice Statistics. Office of Justice Program. *Jail Statistics.* 16 Feb. 2006. 11 Oct. 2006 (http://www.ojp.usdoj.gov/bjs/welcome.html).

Wolf Harlow, Caroline. "Education and Correctional Populations." Abstract. *U.S. Department of Justice Office of Justice Programs Bureau of Justice Statistics Special Report* (2003).

Writing

Once you have evaluated all your sources and chosen the specific ones you need, you are ready to begin the writing stage of Paper #4. If your readers of Paper #3 (peers and teacher) said that your organization of points supporting your opinion was effective, you may want to keep that same organization for Paper #4. Or you may decide to change that in order to create a stronger argument. Freewriting can help you make that decision.

Freewriting Prompts

1. Has your opinion changed since you did your research? If so, in what way(s)?
2. What are you most concerned about for this paper?
3. Which of your arguments is strongest? Weakest?
4. Do you have enough evidence to support each point?

Now you need to structure this longer, more complex paper. To help you organize your material effectively, and to make sure that you <u>do not</u> write a laundry list paper (intro, summary of source 1, summary of source 2, summary of source 3, conclusion), we ask you to fill in this organizational chart.

ORGANIZATIONAL CHART
(Fill out the bottom of this page **before** you begin the chart)

Main Point 1:	Main Point 2:	Main Point 3:	Main Point 4:
Sources:	Sources:	Sources:	Sources:

Under Main Points: In sentence format, state a main point that supports your thesis.
Under Sources: List the source/s that you will use to support each main point. Include the title, author, page number, and type of source (book article, newspaper article, journal article, website, interview, transcript, etc.)

Student: _____

Topic: _____

Controlling Thesis: _____

_____

Now you are ready to draft Paper #4.

Paper #4: The Research Paper

Rough Draft Due _____

Conference Date _____

Final (Revised) Draft Due _____

Assignment

- The research paper is a position paper, a formal argument using a *minimum of three credible sources,* parenthetical citation and documentation. It is based on the topic you chose for your non-researched opinion/position paper and incorporates sources you will locate during our library visit and on your own. This paper utilizes three drafts: one with peer response, one with teacher feedback, and one to be graded.
- Length requirement: 4–6 pages long (no paper shorter than 4 pages will be read)
- This paper must contain MLA parenthetical citations for all source references (see the Hacker style manual) and must have a "Works Cited" page with all sources listed in MLA format.
- Accompanying your paper will be an annotated bibliography. This will be discussed in class.

Format

Use word processing, double spacing, twelve-point font, (Times or Times New Roman,) and standard 1" margins.

You will need a folder for this paper and each document should be in this order:

1. (On top) Final Draft
2. Annotated Bibliography
3. Teacher-Response Draft
4. Peer-Response Drafts (2)
5. Peer Response Handouts (2)
6. Copies of all the sources cited in your paper (articles, etc.)

Note: No source should appear in the "Works Cited" list unless it is cited in your paper.

- ☐ Clearly state your position on the controversial issue discussed in your opinion paper.
- ☐ Find at least three credible sources to support your argument. *Only one of these can be from a credible source on the Internet.*
- ☐ Evaluate your sources by using the questions provided earlier in this chapter.
- ☐ Read and write notes about your sources
- ☐ Develop relationships between your sources
- ☐ Rework your thesis statement if needed
- ☐ Write the rough draft
- ☐ Conference
- ☐ Revision/Rewrite
- ☐ Peer-edit
- ☐ Turn in final draft with all research materials, drafts, articles, etc. in your folder.

As always, we include a list of in-class and out-of-class activities to help you successfully complete the formal argument paper. These exercises appear in the same order as your checklist.

One of the greatest problems students have is integrating research material into their own texts because a smooth transition from your writing to someone else's and back again is not always easy to accomplish. There are, however, a number of techniques you can choose from when you are first learning this practice. The following exercise introduces these techniques and provides places for you to practice them.

Integrating Research

Original Quote:

"Baby sign language has been around for decades, but it has exploded in popularity in recent years, said Jenny Christianson, a family life educator with Sanford Children's CHILD Services. There's a variety of programs or versions of baby sign language, but most teach adapted American Sign Language to hearing infants."
"Parents Help Children Communicate Needs Through Sign Language"
    (par. 5)

There are many ways to integrate research into your paper:

Author named in a signal phrase:

According to Jennifer Gerrietts of <u>The Argus Leader</u>, "There's a variety of programs or versions of baby sign language, but most teach adapted American Sign Language to hearing infants" (par. 5).

Author not named in a signal phrase:

Apparently, "there's a variety of programs or versions of baby sign language, but most teach adapted American Sign Language to hearing infants" (Gerrietts par. 5).

One person quoted by another:

According to Jenny Christianson, a family life educator with Sanford Children's CHILD Services, "baby sign language has been around for decades, but it has exploded in popularity in recent years" (qtd. in Gerrietts par. 5).

Block Quotation:

Jennifer Gerrietts of <u>The Argus Leader</u> writes of how signing to babies has enjoyed a recent revival:
> *Baby sign language has been around for decades, but it has exploded in popularity in recent years, said Jenny Christianson, a family life educator with Sanford Children's CHILD Services. There's a variety of programs or versions of baby sign language, but most teach adapted American Sign Language to hearing infants. (par. 5)*

(This could also be done without naming the author in a signal phrase if you add her name to the citation.)

Summarizing or Paraphrasing:

Jennifer Gerrietts writes that baby sign language has been around for a long time but has recently enjoyed a renewal of interest. She continues with though there are many different types of sign, a modified form of American Sign Language is what is usually used with babies (par. 5).

(This also could be done with naming the author in just the citation and not before)

Now It's Your Turn

Below, write an EXACT quotation from one of your sources you are using—or considering using—for your research paper:

Now, try doing three of the techniques discussed in this exercise (one must be summarizing/paraphrasing and one must include a direct quotation) in the spaces below. Indicate what the techniques are on the lines.

_____ :

_____ :

_____ :

Not only must you integrate direct quotes, you must contextualize them within the framework of your text. Because this technique often proves difficult for many students, we include this exercise on integrating and contextualizing quotes:

Integrating and Contextualizing Quotes

When using research, we often use quotes to give our arguments authority. When inserting quotes, you need to tell why the quote is there, how it supports your claim, and what the quote is suggesting. When introducing a quote, you need to make sure that, if a speaker is mentioned, he or she is identified as an expert. This does not take long; simply calling someone an MD (for a medical quote) is enough.

Once the quote is put into the text, you need to cite it, following MLA guidelines. Below are several (fake) examples of how to put quotes into the context of *your* paper.

Topic: Organ Harvesting as Capital Punishment
Quote: "A single healthy human body can save or significantly improve the lives of over three dozen people."

Paragraph:

When considering organ harvesting as a method of capital punishment, it's important to realize just how valuable one human body is. As Ted Nahasamada MD said, "A single healthy human body can save or significantly improve the lives of over three dozen people" (16). A convict has a debt to pay to society. Having taken lives, he should be able to provide for other people, to make reparations. He should have to donate those organs because so many people will benefit from him doing so; that would truly be paying a debt to society.

Works Cited:
Nahasamada, Ted. A Source for Made- up Quotations. New York: Pseudopress, 2037.

Topic: Teachers should be allowed to carry guns in public schools.
Quote: "Students are already armed. Giving the teachers guns just evens the score. If everyone is armed, no one will want to risk getting shot."

Paragraph:

It's too dangerous for some teachers to teach anymore. Many of them are hiding in the teacher's lounge, afraid to go out into the hallways for fear of a student retaliating over a bad grade. But there are ways to even things out. "Students are already armed. Giving the teachers guns just evens the score. If everyone is armed, no one will want to risk getting shot" (Henricks 23). With everyone afraid of getting shot, no one will want to pull out a gun. So the schools will be safer.

Works Cited:
Henricks, Jahosaphat. Guns don't kill people, I do. New York: Psuedopress, 1994.

Topic: Smoking in public.
Quote: "It is unfair to say that a restaurant is a public place. The owners receive no money from the government. They have to pay taxes. They can require a dress code. They have the right to refuse service to anyone. In many cases, you need a reservation just to get in the door. Since they gain no benefits and have the autonomy that a truly

public place, like a library, does not, the government should not be able to tell business owners not to allow smoking."

Paragraph:
    The main crux of the argument in favor of the smoking ban is the idea that smoking should not be allowed in public. But what does "in public" really mean? Maybe restaurants aren't public places. They are privately owned, after all. "It is unfair to say that a restaurant is a public place … Since they gain no benefits and have the autonomy that a truly public place, like a library, does not, the government should not be able to tell business owners not to allow smoking" (King 16). So all these claims that restaurants are public places, and that people should not be allowed to smoke in public, are based on a faulty assumption. Restaurants are not public places.

Works Cited:
King, David. "Why I am right and everyone else is wrong." The Daily Agitator. February 31, 2009.

Now practice this process of contextualizing your quotes so that your reader knows what they mean and why they appear in your paper. Using your own research, complete the following exercise, following the examples just given.

Identify your topic and stance in a single phrase:
Then pick a short quote to illustrate that topic or prove your stance. Quote:

Now write a paragraph around that quote; introduce it, insert it, and then connect it to your topic or point and cite properly:

Finally, create an MLA "Works Cited" entry.

    The alternative to using direct quotes is paraphrasing, or putting someone else's words into your own. This is a tricky process because you cannot use the other person's words or sentence structure without plagiarising), yet you must convey the same meaning for the paraphrase to be effective. To master this practice, students need

- a clear sense of what a paraphrase is and is not
- a clear understanding of the passage they are attempting to paraphrase— (You cannot convey a meaning you don't understand yourself)
- lots of practice

The Art of Paraphrasing

A paraphrase is...

- your own rendition of essential information and ideas expressed by someone else, presented in a new form.
- one legitimate way (when accompanied by accurate documentation) to borrow from a source.
- a more detailed restatement than a summary, which focuses concisely on a single main idea.

Paraphrasing is a valuable skill because...

- It is better than quoting information from an undistinguished passage.
- It helps you control the temptation to quote too much.
- The mental process required for successful paraphrasing helps you to grasp the full meaning of the original.

6 Steps to Effective Paraphrasing

1. Reread the original passage until you understand its full meaning.
2. Set the original aside, and write your paraphrase on a note card.
3. Jot down a few words below your paraphrase to remind you later how you envision using this material. At the top of the note card, write a key word or phrase to indicate the subject of your paraphrase.
4. Check your rendition with the original to make sure that your version accurately expresses all the essential information in a new form.
5. Use quotation marks to identify any unique term or phraseology you have borrowed exactly from the source.
6. Record the source (including the page) on your note card so that you can credit it easily if you decide to incorporate the material into your paper.

Some examples to compare

The original passage:

Students frequently overuse direct quotation in taking notes, and as a result they overuse quotations in the final [research] paper. Probably only about 10% of your final manuscript should appear as directly quoted matter. Therefore, you should strive to limit the amount of exact transcribing of source materials while taking notes. Lester, James D. Writing Research Papers. 2nd ed. (1976): 46-47.

A legitimate paraphrase:

In research papers students often quote excessively, failing to keep quoted material down to a desirable level. Since the problem usually originates during note taking, it is essential to minimize the material recorded verbatim (Lester 46-47).

An acceptable summary:

Students should take just a few notes in direct quotation from sources to help minimize the amount of quoted material in their research papers (Lester 46-47).

A plagiarized version:

Students often use too many direct quotations when they take notes, resulting in too many of them in the final research paper. In fact, probably only about 10% of the final copy should consist of directly quoted material. So it is important to limit the amount of source material copied while taking notes.

Directions: On a separate piece of paper (or below), write a paraphrase of each of the following passages. Try not to look back at the original passage.

1. The twenties were the years when drinking was against the law, and the law was a bad joke because everyone knew of a local bar where liquor could be had. They were the years when organized crime ruled the cities, and the police seemed powerless to do anything against it. Classical music was forgotten while jazz spread throughout the land, and men like Bix Beiderbecke, Louis Armstrong, and Count Basie became the heroes of the young. The flapper was born in the twenties, and with her bobbed hair and short skirts, she symbolized, perhaps more than anyone or anything else, America's break with the past. From Kathleen Yancey, <u>English 102 Supplemental Guide</u> (1989): 25.

2. Of the more than 1000 bicycling deaths each year, three-fourths are caused by head injuries. Half of those killed are school-age children. One study concluded that wearing a bike helmet can reduce the risk of head injury by 85 %. In an accident, a bike helmet absorbs the shock and cushions the head. From "Bike Helmets: Unused Lifesavers," <u>Consumer Reports</u> (May 1990): 348.

3. While the Sears Tower is arguably the greatest achievement in skyscraper engineering so far, it's unlikely that architects and engineers have abandoned the quest for the world's tallest building. The question is: Just how high can a building go? Structural engineer William LeMessurier has designed a skyscraper nearly one-half mile high, twice as tall as the Sears Tower. And architect Robert Sobel claims that existing technology could produce a 500-story building. From Ron Bachman, "Reaching for the Sky." <u>Dial</u> (May 1990): 15.

When writing a documented formal argument, writers have to know and avoid logical fallacies that can torpedo their points and sink their causes. In formal debates, teams are taught to recognize and pounce upon such fallacies. To help you avoid these pitfalls in your own argument and recognize them in the arguments of others, we include here a list of the most commonly used fallacies:

Six and a Half Basic Fallacies to Avoid

1. Ad hominem: Literally "against the person." This is when, instead of attacking a person's position, you attack the person who is taking the position. For example: "Of course you think abortion is wrong. You're a priest." Or "If you think airport security is too harsh, then you must support the terrorists." This abandons any attempt at reason and is just a personal attack on the opposing side.

2. Appeal to belief: Using as support for an argument the fact that many people believe a thing is true. Just because many people believe a thing does not make that thing true. Many people believed the Earth was flat, but that didn't make it so. If everyone believed the sky was yellow (with the word still meaning what it means now), it would still be blue.

3. Begging the question: Assuming premises that make the conclusion true. Usually a circular form of reasoning. The best example is the Bible: "I know the bible is true because God wrote it. And I know God wrote it because the bible says so." The trouble is that this argument assumes the conclusion is true before presenting it. This can often be very subtle.

4. Slippery slope: An argument that suggests that, if one event happens, others will inevitably follow. This argument is fallacious because there is no guarantee that these other events will follow. For example, take the outdated domino theory of the 1960s and 1970s. "If Vietnam falls, we will lose all of Asia to Communism." Not true. Vietnam fell. The neighboring countries did not go Communist. This is a very common mode of debate in politics. Any argument that leads to chaos, anarchy, or the end of the world is usually the result of a slippery slope fallacy.

5. Straw Man: Ignoring the opposition's actual stance and instead setting up something similar to what they are claiming that is incredibly easy to defeat, and attacking that easily defeatable thing. A claim of victory over that 'straw man' is then used to claim victory over the other side generally. For example: "Abortion is killing a defenseless human being. It's killing an unborn child. Murdering children is obviously a bad thing. So abortion is wrong." Or "My opponent opposes laws that allow the government to arrest people without cause. Do you want someone so willing to let the terrorists come into your town representing you in Washington?" Probably the most common form of 'debate' used in mudslinging campaign commercials.

6. Appeal to the universal: While not technically a fallacy, this practice often leads to problems in any argument. Whenever a universal claim is made (every human being has two arms), it is often believed that the claim is stronger because of its universality. But disproving a universal claim is incredibly easy. Since only one counter example is needed in order to prove the argument wrong, using a universal claim is actually a very weak method of arguing. For the above example, consider the case of a single amputee or child born without an arm. This fallacy is also sometimes labeled an unsupportable generalization.

7. Burden of proof: Rather than proving an argument, using the lack of proof against it as an argument. "No one can show that guns cause crime, so there shouldn't be gun control" may seem to be convincing. But no one would believe "Since no one has proven that there isn't a giant invisible spaghetti monster in the sky, there must be one."

For more examples of fallacies, see http://www.nizkor.org/features/fallacies/

Rhetorical Appeals

While logical fallacies are the negative side of the rhetorical coin and should be avoided at all costs, legitimate rhetorical appeal strategies are the positive side and will, when properly used, strengthen your arguments and help you to convince others of your position. Understanding those appeals will enable you to write a stronger, more effective argument.

Rhetoric is the conscious use of language to influence and convince audiences of the speaker/writer's position on a given issue. Therefore, in argumentative writing, since the goal is to persuade audiences that your position is valid and correct, it is essential that you choose effective words and phrases and organize them in a particular order to convince your audience to agree with you. The Greek philosopher Aristotle designated three means or appeals—*ethos, pathos,* and *logos*—to help you employ tactics that catch an audience's attention and elicit from them potential support for your position. Understanding these three appeals and being able to use them in your own writing will greatly increase your persuasive ability.

Ethos is an appeal to authority and persuades a listener/reader by the writer's character or expertise. When individuals are recognized authorities on particular subjects, they automatically gain the attention and respect of their audiences. For example, a former general has authority to speak on troop movements or weapons deployment; a basketball star like Michael Jordan is recognized as an expert in athletic footwear; and a successful screen actress would be an effective spokesperson for endorsing a line of makeup. On the other hand, the actress would not be given credence if she spoke on military matters nor would anyone listen to a general endorsing basketball shoes because neither have expertise in those areas. The sources you choose should be recognized authorities or experts in the area they are discussing.

Pathos is an appeal to the emotions of an audience. Diction (word choice) and style (the way you put sentences together) affect a listener/reader's emotional response, and when used effectively, these writing choices can help persuade an audience of your argumentative position. As an example, think about a sermon delivered on Sunday from a pulpit, an editorial in a newspaper, or a political speech on television. The minister, the editor and the politician all have one thing in common: they carefully choose what they say and how they say it to influence the thought and/or behavior of their respective audiences. As a writer in a real situation, think about the audience for your paper and choose words and phrases that will "touch" them – get their attention and move them to accept your position.

Logos is an appeal to logical thinking. In order to effectively argue a position and persuade your audience to accept it, you must employ valid reasoning in your paper. Create a clear and complete thesis and support it with plenty of substantial evidence and well-developed points arranged in an effective order, one that progresses logically from point to point and one that links all points back to that original thesis. Think of

continues

Rhetorical Appeals (*Continued*)

a prosecutor or defense attorney addressing a jury. Not only do they bring up as many points as possible to convict or acquit the accused, they present them in a logical order so that the jury can easily follow the development of their argument. That's what you need to do in your own argumentative writing.

People who anticipate the opposition to their positions write the strongest arguments because they take that opposition into consideration while constructing their own points. Sometimes visualizing the opposing side is hard for students who feel strongly about their own position on the issue at hand. In class role playing can help the students "see" the opposition and deal with it effectively.

The Hot Seat

Ask for student volunteers to take "the hot seat" next class to defend their positions in the papers they are currently writing. Volunteers then tell the class their issues and thesis statements. The rest of the class should write down each issue and thesis and consider opposing views (counterarguments) for the next class.

This role playing exercise is meant to help you develop the opposition in your papers. To write a really strong argument, you have to remember that not everyone agrees with you. To convince those who disagree, you must demonstrate to them that their counter-arguments are not as strong as your arguments. To do that, you must anticipate those counter-arguments.

Taking the hot seat enables you to learn what the counterpoints are and gives you a chance to refute them. When a volunteer sits in the "hot seat" in the middle of the room, the rest of the class will fire their counter-arguments at you one at a time. Argue against the ones you can and note the rest so that you can deal with them in your paper.

The Press Conference

As either an alternative or reinforcement for the Hot Seat and another chance for you to practice your argumentative skills, you can participate in a classroom version of a press conference.

In class volunteer students take turns being the "interviewee" while the rest of the class take on the roles of reporters doing the interviewing.

- If you are the interviewee, you already have your thesis and your research. Now it is time to share that material with your classmates.
- Think of any press conference you have ever seen on television. The person being interviewed always makes a brief statement first and then takes questions, one at a time, from the reporters present.
- With this in mind, create a four- or five-minute presentation of your subject, your position and the reasons you hold it. Pretend that the class is the press core and you are addressing those reporters. Clearly state your position and your arguments for it, supporting those arguments with the material from your research.
- Be prepared to answer questions.

For the "reporters:

- Listen carefully to the presentation.
- Take notes just as real reporters do during a press conference.
- From these notes, create at least two questions to ask the writer at the end of the presentation.

Everyone will get a chance to ask a question. That's why you need to create two; someone else might steal your thunder and ask your question before you get a chance to.

As you write your argument, remember that *tone* is key to convincing others. Respect the opinions of those who disagree. To ensure that you maintain a positive and effective tone throughout your paper, complete the following exercise:

Take a Walk in Someone Else's Shoes

Not everyone agrees with you, and it's important to look at things from their side as well as your own. To learn how to do this, take your rough draft and trade it with someone else in the class.

Now that you have someone else's paper, read it. Don't read it to improve it or to find mistakes. Read it just to see their point of view. See what the person is saying and what side he or she is on.

Now write a response to the paper. But do it from the opposite side. Disagree with everything the person said. Remember to respond to each argument. What is wrong with those arguments? What arguments didn't the original writer make? What arguments can you make from your new side? Write this response in as much detail as possible

Give the response to the person whose paper you have.

Now read their response to your paper. How is it worded? Are you insulted by this response? Does it make you angry? Do you have any reason or desire to agree with anything this other person said? Are they being condescending? Are they treating you like you're stupid?

If they are, it's because he or she didn't use a friendly tone. Now think about the tone you used when you wrote the response. Were you mean? Were you rude? If you had no reason or desire to agree with the person, does he or she have any reason to agree with you?

When you are writing to someone who disagrees with you, you have to meet half way. Everyone has a reason to believe what they believe. Everyone has a point and a perspective that makes sense personally. Calling the person stupid won't make that person want to listen to you. Would you want to listen to someone who called you stupid? Or would you be more likely to listen to someone who said, "I understand where you're coming from, and you make a lot of good points, but there's something you may not have considered"?

Meet the person half way. Understand where the person is coming from and realize that he or she is not stupid because he or she disagrees with you. Acknowledge that the person has his or her own arguments. These arguments aren't shortsighted. The person is not believing things without a reason. Instead remember that the

continues

Take a Walk in Someone Else's Shoes (*Continued*)

person just has not seen it from your side yet. Show the person your side, but be friendly about it. This isn't about attacking an enemy. It's about making a friend.

You don't talk down to your friends. You don't yell at your friends, and you don't call your friends names. You try to make your friends see things your way. You try to make them like you. That's what you should do with your audience. Make the audience like you.

It will make your paper stronger.

Things to avoid when trying for a friendly tone:

- No intelligent person would disagree…
- It should be obvious that…
- It is unfair that…
- There is no reason that…
- There are no good points the opposition could make…
- It is stupid to think…
- It is insane to believe…

Things to include when trying for a friendly tone:

- Something people may not have considered is…
- While that is a good point, it should also be remembered that…
- There are a lot of good reasons to think that way, but there are some problems . . .

Documenting Sources

The Modern Language Association (MLA) style sheet is used for all papers written in Freshman Composition. The proper citation forms and documentation formats can be found in your *Pocket Style Manual*, 5th edition. It covers

- what to cite
- when to cite
- how to cite
- where to cite

Therefore, this text does not repeat that information. It does, however, provide some hands on practice for citations and documentation. Below is a "puzzle" exercise for practicing works cited entries.

Works Cited Puzzle

Activity Goal: To provide students with practice in creating a Works Cited entry (in the correct order) when provided with all of the information.

1. Create a Works Cited page that has at least ten source entries listed and change the font to approximately 16 or 18.
2. Print out five copies. Taking one of the copies and using scissors, cut each entry from the page until you have ten slips of paper, each with one Works Cited entry.
3. Then take two entries, and cut up each part (so cut after the author's first name, their last name, the title of the book, etc.). After you have cut each of the two Works Cited entries, put them in an envelope. Repeat this for the

remaining Works Cited entries, putting the parts of two entries in an envelope for a total of five envelopes. Put those five envelopes into a bigger envelope and label it Group 1.

4. Repeat steps two through three for the other four copies of the Works Cited
    page.

5. Divide students into groups (four or five groups depending on the class
    size). Each group should have no more than three members. Hand each
    group a big envelope containing the five envelopes that have the parts of
    the Works Cited entries.

6. Instruct students that they are to take one envelope out of the group one
    that you have given them and that referring to their style manual for guid-
    ance, they must put their two entries in that envelope in the correct Works
    Cited entry order and then alphabetize all of the entries (theirs and those of
    their classmates) in order to create a Works Cited page. The team that com-
    pletes the task correctly in the shortest amount of time wins a prize.

Note: While students may not be able to recreate the entry exactly as it was before
(e.g., maybe they get the publishers confused on their two entries), they should be
able to create a correct Works Cited entry with all of the various parts in the right order
and not have any pieces leftover.

*****

The single greatest problem in writing research papers is, and always has been, plagiarism, the most common form of academic dishonesty. To avoid this pitfall and its consequences, students need to know exactly what constitutes plagiarism, and it is the
teacher's responsibility to explain this issue to the entire class. Simply put, *plagiarism is
stealing the words, research data or ideas of others and passing them off as your own.* One of
the best ways to clarify this definition for students is to let them classify common academic paper situations as plagiarism, other academic dishonesty, acceptable passage, or
"other."

The Plagiarism Game (Adapted from Judie Carroll)

This activity could also be done without group work by using the chalkboard or using
poster board. Obviously, you can customize as you wish. Groups of around five or six
people would probably work best if done in groups. Explain the activity and then
allow ten to fifteen minutes to complete it with approximately five to ten minutes for
discussion.

You have a number of cards with different examples on them and groups have
to place these under the correct heading (plagiarism, academic dishonesty, acceptable, or other). Make sure you have a good range of examples. Perhaps use specific
examples from the course textbook or use the ones listed below.

Hopefully this will create discussion and questions over what is/is not acceptable
and give a chance to demonstrate and explain the specifics of the regulations, definitions, and implications of offences as well as good versus bad practices. The interesting thing about the definitions is that it is not always apparent exactly where some of
the examples should be placed and in some cases, they might go into a number of

continues

The Plagiarism Game (Adapted from Judie Carroll) (Continued)

categories depending on the context. Part of the point of this activity is that it is often difficult for teachers to even decide what category something can go in and that this can be confusing, which is why we talk about it in class.

Here are examples on what you could put on your cards:

- Copying a paragraph from a book without acknowledging the author.
- Copying a paragraph from a book and citing who the author is.
- Taking a crib-sheet into an examination.
- Letting your friend borrow your notes to study for an examination.
- Cutting and pasting a paragraph from an article with a few changes in word order. The paragraph is not in quotation marks, but there is a reference both in-text and in the bibliography.
- Making up quotations.
- Making up fake references.
- Working together with a friend to get ideas for an individual essay and then writing it on your own.
- Taking short phrases from several sources and combing them with phrases of your own to compose a paragraph in your essay. The references are included in the bibliography, but not referenced in the paragraph itself.
- Downloading an essay from a website and handing it in.
- Copying another student's coursework.
- Obtaining and using an essay from a previous year's student.
- Stealing another student's essay and submitting it as your own.
- Submitting an essay as coursework that you have previously used in another class.
- Submitting a jointly written paper as your own.
- Lending another student your coursework to look at.
- Suggesting some useful references to a friend who is struggling with an essay.
- Copying a few sentences from a textbook and putting it in your essay in quotation marks. It is referenced both in text and in the bibliography.
- Not contributing a fair share to group work that is assessed for a group grade.
- Paying someone else to write your essay for you.
- Using someone else's ideas without citing them in the paper or bibliography.
- There are in-text citations but there is no bibliography or works cited page.
- There are in-text citations and there is a bibliography or works cited page.
- Writing an essay for someone else.

Rewriting

This entire assignment has been a major rewrite (revision) of paper #3, the opinion piece. But now that you have a completed draft, it's time to rewrite the rewrite. As always, peer response provides a starting point for beginning draft #2.

Remember, you are the writer; this is *your* paper. Accept or reject advice according to your own best judgment. When in doubt, consult your teacher.

Peer-Editing Paper #4: The Mini-Research Paper

Author's Name _____

Peer-editor's Name_____

Questions from the Writer . . .

Additional questions for the Editors to consider:

Introduction

1. Is the introduction clear? Complete?
   a. Does the author break any of the "Don't" rules that we have discussed previously in class?

2. What additional background information is necessary to set up the paper?

3. **Put a star next to the thesis.**

Organization

4. Mark the transitions between paragraphs.

5. Is anything missing? Should anything be added?

6. Does the writer fully develop her/his position? Make suggestions for further development.

continues

Peer-Editing Paper #4: The Mini-Research Paper (*Continued*)

Detail

7. Are there sufficient details? Find one place that the writer can include more details to enhance the description—put a box around this place. Find one place where the writer uses detail well.

Clarity

8. Mark any confusing passages with wavy lines.
9. Are there distracting surface errors? Do spelling errors or sentence and grammar mistakes interfere with the paper's readability? Remember not to correct them, just answer the question.

10. Find one or two passages you particularly like or that are well-written— and mark them with straight lines.
11. What is the author's message? What is the position?

12. Briefly list the author's supporting points. (There should be at least three.)
   a.

   b.

   c.

   d.

13. What are two questions you still have after reading this paper?
   a.

   b.

REMEMBER:
If you find run-ons, comma splices, grammar errors, spelling errors, etc., just mark them. DO NOT FIX THEM. That's the writer's responsibility, not yours.
   Also, Writers, please remember that peer-editing is one way of getting advice.
   Don't forget that you'll be having a one-on-one conference with me before the final paper is due.
   Use the Writing Center if you want more help. The staff know their stuff and can offer great advice for your papers.

While you are considering your peer response and writing draft #2, consider the following advice:

Good Rules of Thumb for an Argument Paper

1. Be clear. If no one understands what you're trying to say, you won't convince them.
2. Know your audience. Who are you talking to? What are they like?
3. Know your audience's stance. Are you preaching to the choir, or do they disagree with you?
4. Consider the opposition. If you don't pay their arguments any attention, why should they pay yours any?
5. Avoid fallacies. They weaken your argument.
6. Be fair to the opposition. They are not stupid, and they deserve all the respect for their arguments you can give them.
7. Take a stand. Just because you show both sides doesn't mean you aren't taking one.
8. Don't be wishy-washy. Stick firmly to your side, whatever that may be.
9. Be friendly. You attract more flies with honey.
10. Have a hook. Make your reader want to keep reading.
11. Stay on target. Going off on tangents weakens your argument and distracts your reader.

If there is time to do so, you should conference with your teacher with draft #2 to make certain that you have

- written a complete paper—intro, body, conclusion
- arranged points in the best possible order to convince your readers of your position
- provided evidence for every point that you make supporting your thesis
- avoided logical fallacies
- accounted for counter-arguments
- cited every source necessary—quotes, paraphrases, statistics, etc.
- provided a complete works cited page. Nothing cited in the paper should be missing from the Works Cited, and every item in the Works Cited must appear at least once in the paper itself
- cleaned up surface errors and eliminated any deep errors that interfere with meaning

If time is short and conferences are impossible, you can work on your final draft in class in the computer lab while the teacher checks over each one and answers any questions you have.

After this conference or class session, it's time for the second rewrite or third draft, the one you will turn in for a grade.

*****

Process Write for Paper #4, the Mini-Research Paper

Please write about your writing process for Paper #4. **Do this process write outside of class and turn it in [on due date] with your paper and all of its components.** This writing may come in the form of a letter or an essay—whichever is easier for you. Make sure you write on each of the items listed. Absolutely do not give me a list of answers to the prompt questions below. Please elaborate and provide details in your responses. Feel free to mix, match, and rearrange the following prompts as you see fit to help you write this:

- -

1. Why did you choose this topic?
2. Evaluate the research process. What were some of your struggles in researching your topic? What could have made it easier?
3. What did you want to accomplish with this paper? What was your purpose in writing it (other than it was required)? Do you feel you accomplished that purpose?
4. Please reflect on your support material for your paper. Do you think you have sufficient support for your paper? Did you include counterpoints? Do you think they helped support your thesis? How could you have improved? Please explain.
5. In writing this paper, what helped you produce the final draft? Did anyone else help you? If so, who was it and how did he/she/they help you?
6. What are the strengths and weaknesses in your paper? Explain.
7. What do you like best about your paper? Least? Explain.
8. What was the easiest part of writing this paper? The hardest? Explain.
9. What would you do differently if you had the chance to do the paper over? Why?
10. Do you have any final comments?

Don't Forget

On [due date], you must have your paper "ready to turn in" when you come to class; time will not be allowed for in class proofreading or editing – do that before you come to class. **Make sure you bring the following items with you to class on [due date], assembled in a binder, ready to turn in:**

- Process write
- Final draft w/ Works Cited page
- Conferenced draft(s)
- Draft from in class peer response
- copies of sources (or citations and summaries of sources if books, films, or something else that the teacher cannot easily get)

Paper #4 (Mini-Research Paper) Process Questions
WRITE YOUR RESPONSE IN ESSAY FORM!

1. Did you have trouble finding enough information?
2. Did you have any problem arranging your material?
3. Are you satisfied with your paper?
4. Do you have sufficient evidence for each point? Is there any point you need to reinforce? Which one(s) and why?
5. Do you feel you arranged your points in the best possible order to convince your reader?
6. Do you think you did convince/inform your reader?
7. What was the most difficult part of this paper—the process or the actual writing of the paper? If process, what part of the process and why? If the paper, what part and why?
8. How many hours overall did you spend on this project (not counting class time)?
9. Do you feel you spent enough time? Too much?
10. What is the strongest part of your paper? The weakest?
11. If you had to do it over again, what would you do differently and why?

Process Essay Questions for Paper #4, the Mini-Research Paper

Remember, when you're writing the process essay...

- Do not answer the questions in a list, but in a response essay try to cover each idea.
- You may move the questions around as you see fitting, so don't restrict yourself to the question-answer format.
- Be conscientious of your format—12pt Romans/New Times Roman, double-spaced, 1" margins, etc.

1. Explain the organization of your argument. Refer to the flow chart handout.
2. After reviewing your research and organizing your argument, what conclusion(s) did you reach?
3. What one piece of advice (either from a peer-editor, the teacher or the writing center,) helped the most?
4. What do you see as some strengths of this paper? Is there anything in this paper that seems weak to you?

Above are three possible process sheets for this assignment.

Final papers should be submitted in a folder, manila envelope, or expando file. Each folder must contain

- Process sheet on top
- Final draft with Works Cited page
- Notes on teacher feedback that led to final draft
- Peer response handouts and comments that led to draft #2
- Organizational chart
- Copies of all sources cited in your paper with cited passages highlighted

Part Six
The Essay Exam

ASSIGNMENT FIVE: The Essay Exam

While we as writing teachers know that all good writing is rewriting and that redrafting with peer and teacher feedback always produces a better paper, we do recognize that there is one kind of writing that cannot take advantage of these essential processes. By its very nature, the in-class timed essay exam is a one-draft piece that requires you, the student, to produce within a specific time period a coherent, organized paper explaining a particular topic or answering a specific question. There is no time to share with others, receive feedback, and rewrite with your audience in mind. There is only the question that must be answered within the 50- or 75-minute class period.

Regardless of the alien nature of this kind of writing, it is still a part of academic testing and real life work situations, and because it is, we have devised a series of steps you can go through to help you prepare for this kind of writing task. By learning these "secrets of taking an essay exam," you can master this writing task as successfully as you have mastered research and synthesis in papers #3 and #4. In fact, the process of synthesis, incorporating material from numerous sources into one coherent paper, will greatly aid you in incorporating material from your textbook, class lecture notes, and class discussion into your in-class essay.

The Secrets of Taking an Essay Exam

Although the idea of writing a complete, coherent and effective essay "under the gun," so to speak, may seem both difficult and alien from the writing processes we have emphasized throughout this course, it is still a *writing* task and, as such, can be mastered by using a process approach. First divide the process into three chronological segments:

- Before the exam
- During the test itself
- And after you have finished writing

Further dividing each of these three segments into specific linear steps creates a simple effective road map for succeeding on an essay exam.

Before the Exam

Mastering the material for the test involves a number of different learning processes that you have already become familiar with in writing class:

1. a close, careful reading of the texts the test will cover (textbook, lecture notes, group and/or class discussion notes, outside reading assignments),
2. analysis of each of those texts through highlighting, marginal comments, note taking, paraphrasing, etc. (Use the 6 steps for close reading),
3. summarizing those texts after analysis (remembering the seven steps for the summary assignment, Paper #3)
4. synthesizing those summaries into logical groupings (usually chronologically or thematically or both. Other groupings are possible).

Now you have identified the relevant subject matter and become familiar with it; you know what you are going to write about. To master it and feel comfortable dealing with it in various ways, you should now begin to analyze the process of taking the actual exam:

1. Consider your past performance on writing tests and remember that an essay exam tests your KNOWLEDGE, your ABILITY TO THINK (apply that knowledge in specific ways), and your ABILITY TO WRITE (to present those applications clearly, logically, and correctly).
2. Analyze your audience. Look over our notes and journals and think about your observations in class. What did the teacher emphasize, repeat, or dwell on at length?
3. Formulate possible questions. Focus on key concepts you have identified and consider ways you could be questioned about those concepts.
4. Practice writing out answers to find content gaps in your answers. Time yourself and get used to writing within time constraints.
5. Go back over the original summaries and notes and fill in the gaps you discovered in your answers. In other words, stop worrying about what you already know, identify what you don't know, and focus on learning that material.
6. Now formulate new questions and write new answers.
7. Check original texts for essential names, dates, spellings, etc. Facts matter and accuracy counts.

During the Test Itself

1. Read through the entire exam carefully before attempting to answer anything. Underline key directional words like *describe, explain, compare, contrast, defend, dispute*, etc. Determine what the teacher wants you to do before you start to write.
2. Proportion your time. If there are several sections, allot appropriate time to each and follow your schedule. If there is only one question, allow time for generating and organizing material, actually writing the essay, and then checking your piece.
3. Start with the easiest question first. Being able to generate the answer will "warm up" your writing muscles and prepare you to deal effectively with the more difficult questions later. Begin by jotting down all the relevant points you can remember. Number them in the order in which you plan to include them in your answer. This process creates an informal outline for your essay.
4. Now generate an overall thesis, **often restating and then completing the original test question creates just such a thesis**. That statement, plus your number of points, creates the organization of your essay.
5. Write as clearly and correctly as you can. You have no time for a second draft. As you write, if new ideas surface, make a note in the exam margins and try to work those ideas in as you go.

6. Remember to cite specific examples, reasons, evidence to support your points from notes, texts, and discussion just as you did in Paper #4 (except that this time documentation is not required). **To make a statement does not prove it;** provide support for each point you raise.
7. Read over your essay, and neatly make corrections when needed.

After You Have Finished Writing the Essay, Checking It Should Include:
- identifying a clear thesis statement,
- reading for coherent organization,
- checking for support, evidence,
- seeing if you provided independent thought, analysis or argument if the question called for or allowed such originality, and
- making sure that you have a conclusion—an essay exam is still a paper with a beginning, middle, and end. Just don't stop writing; conclude logically. This is often the spot for that originality to emerge. If time expires before you finish, add a note to the teacher that you did not complete your essay. Then at least she knows you know the essay is incomplete.

A few students produce their best writing on the essay exam; the time limit makes them focus and concentrate on organizing their material. But most dread essay exams; they fear writer's block—going blank and staring at the empty white space with no idea how to fill it up. That's why in class practice matters so much in this assignment. Collaboratively students need to go through all the steps involved in "the secrets of taking an essay exam" so that the process becomes an ingrained, almost unconscious part of their writing processes. To accomplish that, each class or each instructor prepares for the exam by going through those steps, one by one, in class together.

The three part generic process outlined here can be condensed into a series of in-class and homework exercises that familiarize you with this process while simultaneously providing you with the materials that you will need for that timed writing task.

- Individual teachers choose a relevant topic that most freshmen can relate to, are at least partially familiar with, or would like to explore and learn about. This section provides four such sample topics with appropriate sources and exercises for each.
- Students read (print sources), watch (TV or film), and/or listen to (recordings of songs, poetry, speeches) the texts that cover this topic and then discuss those texts in detail in class.
- Just as they did in Paper #4, students summarize each source and develop relationships between the sources. For example, a TV episode is an example of the print text article about Civil Rights. Or a film contrasts with the short story about how teens handle peer pressure.

After discussion and exercises have made the class comfortable with the material, students collaboratively generate possible questions for the exam itself. Instructors write these questions on the board, and the students edit and rearrange them to ensure that each is clear and comprehensive. Then they vote on their favorite five or six, write them down and practice answering them in class and at home, using the selected texts as source material. Instructors will pick three of the six as alternate choices for the essay exam without telling the students which three were chosen. By practicing with all six, students not only become familiar with the writing processes involved in taking an essay exam, they "study" the material for the test as well. And they accustom themselves to writing under time constraints.

*****

While there are no set subjects for essay exams, there are topics that have worked well in the recent past. Any topic should encompass at least three sources, multimedia if possible. Here is one such topic and the teaching packet developed to accompany it.

Serial Killers

Possible texts:

From Hell (film about Jack the Ripper)
Monster (film about Aileen Wournos)
Texas Chainsaw Massacre

The New York Times has several articles about serial killers—both recent and historical murders

CSI (Las Vegas)—Episodes "Anonymous" (Season 1, Episode 8) and "Identity Crisis" (Season 2, Episode 13)—both episodes profile the same serial killer "The Miniature Killer" if Season 7 is out on DVD

Dexter (any episode from the series)

For further research, visit http://www.crimelibrary.com/serial_killers/index.html, which has a number of detailed articles about serial killers.

The nice thing about this topic is that you can find articles anywhere on the internet about serial killers. There are also several interesting research papers that can be found through Malpass Library's website (for example, "Kill and Kill Again").

Follow already familiar formats assigning readings as homework, viewing relevant film or TV episodes in class together, and discussing all sources through group work and whole class discussion.

Exercise #1: Summarizing Sources

- Set up round robin collaborative summaries similar to the collaborative narrative in Part II with each of the sources
- Use the lab for "musical computers" or the classroom in a circular configuration
- For the first source, have each student start the summary by writing the introduction
- Then have students pass papers to the left or move over one computer seat and write paragraph #2 using another student's intro
- Have them shift a third time and complete the summary and conclude
- Share these summaries in class, allowing students to take notes to add points others covered that are not in their summaries

or

- Choose the best summary and post it for the class to use
- Repeat this exercise with each source

*****

Role playing is another way to clarify difficult material for students.

Exercise #2—Short Skit

In your group, create a short skit (approximately 15 minutes long) based on your assigned text.

The skit should center around a courtroom setting. There should be two sides—one representing the killer and one representing the victim. You can introduce any number of witnesses. You should review your original source text in order to know your "characters" in depth. Be prepared to answer any questions about your characters. You should be able to "think on your feet."

Be sure to have a written script (just in case one of your "characters" turns up absent and you need someone else to fill in). You will need to type up this script in advance and turn it in after your presentation.

You will need to incorporate at least three of the following questions into your skit:

1. How does law enforcement react to the killings?
2. What are the methods used in each case? (Either how law enforcement caught the killers, or how the killers killed their victims.)
3. How is your killer's physical characteristic portrayed in comparison to "typical" killers?
4. Is there a relationship between the victims? (Is there a reason only certain kinds of people are chosen as victims?)
5. What is the killer's viewpoint in comparison to "typical" killers?
6. How is the killer affected by his or her environment?
7. Has the killer baited the police? If so, how and why?
8. In what era did the killings take place? How does this affect the crime?
9. Does the killer fit the stereotype of a serial killer? (sympathy/empathy?)
10. What defense would the serial killer give in a courtroom setting?

Feel free to "tweak" the questions to fit your skit. In other words, as long as your concept answers the questions in some way (though vague), that is okay.

Make your skits exciting! Think *Law and Order* meets *Jerry Springer* . . .

Once summarizing, discussion, and role playing are complete, you are ready to generate a series of questions for the exam itself. One possible method of developing those questions follows.

Exercise #3

- For homework assign each student the task of writing two possible questions for the next class. Each question must require using at least three sources in its answer.
- Stage an "everybody talks" day. Go around the room and have each student read aloud one of his/her questions.
- Put those questions on the board and let the class choose six, knowing that three of the six will appear on the exam as choices for their essays.

The result of this exercise will be the essay exam itself.

Essay Exam Instructions and Questions

Before you begin, read through all the directions carefully.

You have 50 minutes to write a two to three page paper on one of the following topics. The essay must be at least two whole pages long. Remember to include a title for your essay. Indicate which question you have chosen in the heading.

Joe Moe
Question 1
April 19, 2009

Your Clever and Unique Title

Remember, you are allowed to bring in only one page (one side) of notes. Staple your notes to your completed essay before you turn it in.

Good luck!

1. What drove the serial killers to commit their crimes? Are these motives related to or driven by past/childhood occurrences? Give three examples of serial killers and their motives.
2. Compare and contrast three serial killers and how they were portrayed by members of society.
3. Why do you think people are so interested in serial killers? What makes killers "attractive" for newspapers, television and even personal gossip? Name at least three serial killers and why society might find them interesting.

Two Sample Student Papers

Paper 1

Chris Mortimer
Question 3
April 19, 2009

Infatuation Nation: Serial Killers

Extra! Extra! Read all about it, serial killer strikes again. These words though not used by the paperboy selling papers attract attention each and every single time a serial killer is on the loose. What is it that makes Americans have such an attraction to those who kill their victims in such a slow and horrible death? Ever since serial killers have struck the media has been fascinated with serial killers. Why is this and who does society find interesting? What makes a popular serial killer compared to boring serial killers? No one may know the complete answer but I think it may have to do how closely the person related to normal society.

America's fascination with serial killers may seem odd and strange but when looking at the psyche of American people it sort of makes sense. Americans are always buying the tabloids with fresh stories about the fallout of a celebrity's marriage, which one is in drug rehab now. Americans are fascinated towards a life they themselves do not lead or understand. When people watch their nightly news and see the top story of a serial killer on the loose they become intrigued. They become intrigued because they wonder what is going on in the murderer's head. They are wondering what could drive a human being to hate. They are wondering how someone could possibly conceive to commit this act. Whether it is mutilation towards the victim or rape? People are interested because the killer seemed to live a normal life, they seemed to have it all and then they snapped. This can be seen in one serial killer's story.

John Wayne Gacy was one of these killers mentioned above. John had it all. John did have a not-so-nice childhood, but it seemed that he had overcome that. He had grown up in a blue collar family with an abusive alcoholic father. That did not deter Gacy from become a well-known liked individual of suburbia life. John was a member of the Junior Chamber of Commerce in Des Plaines, Illinois. He was also a clown at the neighborhood parties and a precinct captain in the local Democratic Party, plus he owned his own contraction business. John had it all, but then he did not. He seemed to be fighting demons in his head until he finally let them loose. John Wayne Gacy killed, murdered and tortured 32 men. John described to the police how he would kill them by strangling them while raping them as well. John would also keep the bodies under his bed sometimes for several hours until moving them to the crawl space. This case really incensed average Americans. They become worried because a man with so much potential and so much going for him just had snapped. John was an average American who killed 32 people, if that does not grab someone's attention I don't know what will, maybe the next story.

Albert Fish was one of the most sadistic killers of all times. You may not have heard of him but people back in the earliest 20th century sure did. Fish was a sado-masochist who would inflict pain onto himself. Fish would stick himself with needles or light himself on fire. He would target poor families and then murder their sons. He would rape them, torture them with many different "instruments of Hell" and then slowly kill them. Fish was sadistic as it came and was relentless. Finally when caught he tried to use the insanity plea saying the voices in his head had told him to kill the innocent children. He was executed less than one year after his trail. Why would this attract media and public attention? It would because it is not everyday news having a serial killer who performs these horrific acts. Sometimes it may not be that act that is interesting but who is doing it.

Aileen Wournos born in Rochester, Michigan was considered to be one of the first and deadliest female serial killer. Aileen was considered to be quite a character; from the moment of her first killing to her execution. She had grown up in a bad childhood with a molesting father and a deserting mother. Aileen became pregnant at the age of 14, presumably with her brother's child and was kicked out of her grandparent house. Aileen admitted to killing seven men in many different instances, but she never really tortured them like other serial killers. Aileen had used the self defense routine in her trial saying that even though she was a prostitute her first victim tried to rape her so she killed him. This was widely disputed and eventually led her to her guilty verdict. Though surprisingly the police did not ever find a rape charge against Aileen's first victim a reporter did after running his name through the FBI database. Aileen was found guilty of murder and was sentenced to death by lethal injection. Aileen never

continues

Infatuation Nation: Serial Killers (*Continued*)

said she was crazy and became very irritated when people would say she was. She is quoted as saying, "I killed those men, robbed them cold as ice. And I'd do it again, too. There's no chance in keeping me alive or anything, because I'd kill again. I have hate crawling through my system . . . I am so sick of hearing this 'she's crazy' stuff. I've been evaluated so many times. I'm competent, sane, and I'm trying to tell the truth. I'm the one who seriously hates human life and I would kill again." Aileen was executed shortly after, but before her execution was stayed so they could complete one more round of psyche evaluations. Aileen Wournos may not have tortured her victims like the others, but she still killed.

What is it that attracts us to the lives of Serial Killers? What is it that makes us so interested in the horrible awful lives of other individuals? Could it be that we are bored of our own life or we need some excitement? I am not sure (a psychologist may know), but this is what I do know: there are people out there, who do bad things and those bad things excite people. They excite people enough to wonder what if. What if I did that? What if that happened in my family? What if it happened to me? The unknown fascinates people and that what makes me think they like serial killers. No one really knows what's going on in the mind of a serial killer. No one really knows where the killer is or where they will strike next. All they know is that it excites them and they cannot turn off the television.

Sample Student Paper 2

Erin Hoppman
Question 1
April 19, 2009

From Baby to Gruesome Serial Killer

Many people have often wondered what drives serial killers to commit the gruesome acts they are charged with. The most common factor that many serial killers have in common is a rough and often abusive past or childhood. Every human being is born as an innocent little baby, but as time goes on each child is raised differently and has many different experiences. These experiences, good or bad, often determine what kind of person he will be as an adult. After reading about three different serial killers, such as John Wayne Gacy, Albert Fish, and Aileen Wournos, I have determined that their childhood experiences were the main contribution to their adult lives as serial killers.

According to the article "Boy Killer: John Wayne Gacy", John Wayne Gacy was a middle child born in Chicago in 1942 to a typical blue-collar family. He had a pretty normal childhood except for the relationship he had with his father. His father was an unpleasant, abusive alcoholic who often physically and verbally abused Gacy. Gacy wanted to gain his father's attention and approval very desperately, but failed. When he was eleven years old he was struck in the head with a playground swing and suffered from blackouts until the age of sixteen. Doctors corrected his condition with medication after they diagnosed him with a blood clot on his brain.

Although the blood clot was removed, the pain and emotional scars of the abuse he endured from his father led to Gacy's life as a vicious serial killer. One of the worst things about Gacy was that to society he seemed like a normal guy. He was a respected member of Junior Chamber of Commerce, a clown at children's parties, a precinct captain in the local Democratic Party, and the owner of his own contracting company.

Because of his roles in society, people tended to trust him very much. With this trust, it made it easily possible to kill and go unnoticed. His biggest way to kill was to lure his victims into being handcuffed to show them "a trick pair of handcuffs" that he used in his clown act. Once cuffed, he killed his victims by pulling a rope or board against their throats as he raped them. After they were dead he would put them in a crawl space under his home. Gacy ended up killing thirty-three youths throughout his lifetime. All of these deaths were directly related to the pain he endured as a child.

According to the article "Albert Fish," who was another serial killer, was born Hamilton Fish on May 19, 1870 to parents from a family with a long history of severe mental illness. He was sent away to an orphanage where he endured severe beatings and whippings. Later on he would admit that he was the only child at the orphanage who actually enjoyed the beatings. In 1890, he moved to New York City and raped children and committed very bizarre sexual acts. He finally married a woman in 1898 and had six kids. Ironically, his children went on to live very normal lives, except for the time where Fish asked his children to spank him with a paddle that contained very sharp nails. The abuse from his childhood was so intense that it led to him inflicting huge amounts of pain on many other people.

Because he was a painter, he traveled around the United States. Fish admitted that he killed one person in every sate he visited. It is no surprise that Fish was considered a sadomasochist, which is a person who derives sexual pleasure from receiving and exerting pain. Each child he kidnapped was tied up and whipped with a belt covered in nails. He also liked to eat the flesh, urine and feces of his victims. Not only did Fish love to inflict harm on others but he often mutilated himself by sticking needles into his skin and lighting himself on fire as well. If Fish would not have been abused so much as a child, he would not have grown up thinking that was the right thing to do. Because he was abused as a child, he was basically taught that abuse is right and that is what an adult is supposed to do with a child.

Along with Fish and Gacy, another serial killer fits the mold as an abused youth who grew up to be a heinous serial killer. According to the article "Aileen Wournos", Aileen was born on February 29, 1956 as Aileen Pittman. Her parents separated months before she was born and her father ended up serving time in mental hospitals as a deranged child molester. Her mother left her and her brother, Keith, in the care of Aileen's grandparents and described them as "crying, unhappy babies". Eventually the grandparents ended up adopting Aileen and Keith as their own. When she was six, Aileen suffered scarring facial burns while she and Keith were setting fires with lighter fluid. Obviously there was something wrong with her mind if she was getting a thrill out of setting fires at the mere age of six.

Aileen eventually dropped out of school and became a teenage hooker and moved across the United States as she pleased. This is where she was able to meet most of her future victims. Aileen went by many different aliases, such as Sandra Kretsch, Lori Grody, Susan Blahovec, Cammie Marsh Green, and Lee Blahovec. She would kill her victims by shooting them in the chest multiple times with a .22 pistol. After they were dead, she would steal their valuables and pawn them off for extra money. When police finally caught Aileen, it was her lesbian lover, Tyria Moore, who pleaded with her to confess to the crimes. She eventually confessed to six killings, but claimed they were all in self-defense.

continues

From Baby to Gruesome Serial Killer (*Continued*)

Obviously Aileen, like both Fish and Gacy, is nothing close to normal. All three suffered from great abuse, awful experiences, and even horrible ruthless parents. All children are very naïve and believe almost everything they are told. They grow up watching the acts of others around them, which is usually their parents. Children usually see their parents as all-knowing gods and imitate their actions. Because of these serial killers horrible parents and the pain they endured, all three grew up believing this was the right way to do things in life. These beliefs, in return, caused the killers to go on and inflict great amounts of pain on many people throughout their lives.

Fairy Tales, Old and New

Brothers' Grimm "Cinderella"
Disney's animated film "Cinderella"
Film "Shrek"
J.R.R. Tolkien's essay "On Fairy-Stories" (summary only):
http:larsen-family.us/~1066/onfairystories.html

Reading, summarizing, discussing, and working with the texts is always the first segment. This example, like all topics, would follow the generic pattern of development but, because different topics engender different exercises, we include here only the ones that differ from the first sample.

Freewrite on characteristics of a fairy tale. Include

- what makes a story a fairy tale?
- what are the characteristics of a fairy tale?
- what kind of characters appear in almost all fairy tales?

In groups of four, share the responses and collaboratively write a definition of a fairy tale. Each group shares their definition with the whole class. The class collaboratively creates a complete definition from the group products. Everyone takes notes on final product. This definition, complete with characteristics, becomes one of the sources for Paper #5.

Compare the class' characteristics with Tolkien's. Combine and create one master list.

Then watch Disney's "Cinderella" in class after reading the Brothers Grimm's story. Using Tolkien's essay, discuss each in turn, focusing on how each does or doesn't fit Tolkien's and the class parameters.

Finally watch "Shrek" as a class. During the viewing, students should

- look for and list evidence that supports "Shrek" being characterized as a fairy tale
- look for and list evidence that goes against the definition of a fairy tale

Discuss results in class.

Essay Exam Instructions and Questions

You have 50 minutes to write a two- to three-page paper on one of the following topics. Remember to include a title for your essay. Indicate which question you have chosen in the heading.

For example:

Joe Moe
Question 1
April 18, 2009

Clever and Unique Title

Remember, your index/note card must be 3 x 5—no bigger. Staple your card to your completed essay.

Good luck!

1. Does Shrek follow the conventions of fairy story? Or does it deviate from them? Use Tolkien's terms and specific examples from Shrek (and Cinderella) to defend your answer.
2. How do the characters in Cinderella and Shrek reflect Tolkien's ideas? (Remember to include discussion of villains.)
3. Compare the Brothers Grimm Cinderella and Shrek using Tolkien's terms. How are they different? The same? Is one more relevant to you than the other? Why?
4. Compare the Prince and Shrek, and compare Cinderella and Fiona in terms of the traits of heroines, damsels in distress, etc.

A Third Possible Topic:

Life Choices: (use multimedia sources and follow the pattern of first two topics)
"The Road Not Taken"—poem by Robert Frost
Felicity—use TV series pilot episode
"Just Breathe"—song by Anna Nalick
"The Lady or the Tiger"—short story by Frank R. Stockton
Stand by Me—film

One different exercise involves an in-class participatory physical activity to help you decode the most difficult of these texts, Frost's enigmatic poem. Its concept and format can be adapted for other obtuse texts.

Essay Exam—"Choice" Theme
Interpreting Text #1, Road Trip Activity

After critically reading and, if possible, listening to Robert Frost's "The Road Not Taken," perform the following classroom activity while keeping the poem in mind.

Set up: Students should arrange their desks in a circle around the mapped out "road trip" cards on the floor. After choosing one student volunteer, half of the circle is assigned the role of that student's "family," and the other half represents the student's "friends."

Student volunteer:

3. Flip over the "start" card in order to read the described "choice" aloud to your peers.
4. You now have two choices in front of you. The card you have flipped over allows you to go to the left (choice #1) or go to the right (choice #2).
5. You can consult with your family or friends, or you can decide for yourself. Contemplate this decision aloud.
6. After deciding which direction you want to take, step towards that card, and flip it over to find out the result of your choice.
7. With each card you flip over, you'll have more decisions to consider and different paths to take. Repeat the previous steps for each card until you've reached the end of the "road trip."
8. Now, looking back at the path you have taken, do you have any regrets? Knowing the outcome, are there any decisions you wish you wouldn't have made? Any turns you wish you would've made?

Aspects of activity and poem to discuss:

5. Now that you have, in a sense, acted out Frost's poem, do you think "The Road Not Taken" is about regret?
6. As Frost, or the poem's main character, looks back over his road, do you think he is feeling positive or negative? How do you feel as you look back at your own roads in life?
7. Are there such things as right and wrong choices?
8. How have different life experiences, or road blocks, shaped who you are as a person?
9. What is more important, the destination or the path?

Road Trip Activity Setup

Cards:

"Start" = You're a freshman in high school, and your parents decide to get a divorce. Your father, who used to work in an office all day long, has decided to move to a small farm in Indiana, and your mother is staying in Illinois. You have to make a choice: where are you going to live?

Choices: 1A = Indiana
1B = Illinois

1A (Indiana) = It's difficult at first, but, as time passes, you have real conversations with your dad and get to know each other. Two years later, he dies of cancer. If you had stayed in Illinois, you may never have had the chance to get to know your father.

You spent a lot of time at the hospital during your father's treatments. As you saw the number of patients who were helped, you became interested in medicine. Proceed to 2A.

1B (Illinois) = Your mom starts dating right away, and you butt heads with the new man in her life. To get away from the situation, you join a local church youth group. The summer after your sophomore year, you make plans to take a vacation with your friends to Florida. After you make these plans, you find out about a church missionary trip to Africa. Where do you want to go?
Choices: 2B = Florida
2C = Africa

2A = Even after your father's death, you continue to stay in touch with many of the doctors and nurses at the hospital. They inform you about a summer internship program for high school students interested in becoming doctors. The internship program is in New York City. In order to go, you would have to sell your father's farm. If you don't go, you'll spend the summer working on the farm until you decide what to do with it. What do you want to do?
Choices: 3A = Farm
3B = New York City

2B (Florida) = On the plane ride to Florida you sit next to a 40-year-old man who is terrified of flying. The other passengers ignore him and your friends are laughing at him, but you decide to talk to him, helping him to feel more comfortable. Once you land, the man, in gratitude, gives you his business card. He's the Dean at the University of Florida. He says to give him a call once you're ready to choose a college. Move on to 3C.

2C (Africa) = In Africa, you make some lifelong friends, Harry, Kendra, and Lee. The four of you work together to build a new school house. Once the structure is in place, you meet with a group of orphaned African children who will be studying in it. You're amazed by their gratitude, selflessness, and happiness. It's difficult to leave at the end of the summer, but you know you will never forget the experience.

3A (Farm) = The work is hard, and the summer is hot. Frustrated by a broken tractor, you drive into town to buy some parts. The 18-year-old behind the counter goes to the farm to take a look at the problem and is able to fix it. You start to fall for this person and spend the rest of the summer side by side. It is arguably the best summer of your life. Move on to 4A.

3B (NY) = You're by yourself in the largest city in the nation and feel completely alone and overwhelmed. The internship program is grueling. While you're still interested in pursuing medicine, you're not sure if you can handle the pressure.

By the end of the summer, however, you have learned that you can make it on your own—a lesson that will come in handy later in life. Move on to 4B.

3C = Five years later, the Dean you met on the plane arranged for you to attend University of Colorado, where you recently graduated with a degree in business. You accept the first job you're offered, a marketing position at an advertising firm. Proceed to 4C.

continues

Essay Exam—"Choice" Theme
Interpreting Text #1, Road Trip Activity (*Continued*)

3D = Five years later, after your missionary trip to Africa, you graduated from a local college with a degree in sociology and became a social worker.

You've been dating your co-worker for the past six months and have decided to get married. Move on to 4D.

4A = The summer ends and so does your romance. By this time, your uncle has decided to take over the farm.

Seven years later, you've graduated college and are now working in agricultural sales. You feel like you have almost everything except someone to share it with. As you're walking down the street, you notice somebody you're interested in. Do you stop this person and ask for the stranger's phone number?
>   Choices: 5A = Ask for phone number
>   5B = Keep walking

4B = Ten years later, deciding that becoming a doctor is not for you, you instead pursued a graduate degree and became a teacher. Your job is demanding, and you put your students first. One night you're rushing to finish writing an exam, and you have intense stomach pains as well as headaches. Do you brush it off, or do you go to the doctor?
>   Choices: 5C = Brush it off
>   5D = Go to doctor

4C = In your first year, you're making $63,000, but you're miserable. The hours are long, your boss is a jerk, and the work is boring. As you're sitting in a meeting, you have an overwhelming gut feeling that you should not stay in this job.

Do you quit that day, or do you stay in your safe, secure job?
>   Choices: 5E = Stay
>   5F = Quit

4D = Six months later, you've had a sick to your stomach, gut feeling that your engagement is a mistake. You've seen characteristics in your fiancé that alarm you.

When you're having dinner at a local restaurant, your fiancé is incredibly rude to, and impatient with, the waitress. Your fiancé also makes some discriminatory comments that you firmly disagree with. It's a week before your $10,000 wedding. The invitations have already gone out. Do you call it off?
>   Choices: 5G = Go through with it
>   5H = Call it off

5A (Ask for number) = Your courage pays off. Not only do you get the phone number, but, after one and a half years of dating, you decide to get married. The two of you live on a farm together and eventually have three children.

5B (Keep walking) = You tell yourself that the stranger would just laugh at you, and you walk right by. As you continue on through the town square, you notice a stranded dog and decide to take him home. Although you missed an opportunity to meet someone, you did find a best friend.

5C (Brush off) = Refusing to go to the doctor, you continue to live your life as is and put your students first. In another three years, however, you die of a rare disease that went undiagnosed because you never went to the doctor.

5D (Doctor) = You find out that you have a rare, but treatable, disease. After spending months in the hospital for treatments, you get to know a cancer patient in the room next to you. Although this person has a terminal illness, you fall in love and decide to get married.

5E (Stay) = While your salary goes up each year, your quality of life goes down. However, everything changes in about six years. After gaining the necessary lower-level experience, you receive and accept a new job offer from a different company. Although you feel as though you lost the past six years of your life, you love your new job/position.

5F (Quit) = For the first time in your life, you take a chance. With no idea what you'll do, you quit your job. It is both frightening and liberating. You have no idea what you're going to live off of, but you also feel excited about choosing something new to pursue.

5G (Do it) = You tell yourself it's just cold feet, and you go through with the wedding. Ten years later, you find out that your spouse has cheated on you.

5H (Call off) = While many are shocked, your closest friends from the Africa trip—Harry, Kendra, and Lee—come to your rescue. The four of you decide to take a second trip to Africa.

Physical Setup

H	5G	5F	5E	5D	5C	5B	5A
Call it off	Go through with it	Quit	Stay	Go to doctor	Brush it off	Keep walking	Ask for #

4D	4C	4B	4A
6 months later	1st year of work	10 years later	7 years later

3D	3C	3B	3A
5 years later	5 years later	NYC Internship	Farm

2C	2B	2A
Africa	Florida	Continue

1B	1A
Illinois	Indiana

Start

Other possibilities:
Three versions of the same story

Charles Dickens' *A Christmas Carol*
and two film's
Scrooged with Bill Murray
Ms. Scrooge with Cicely Tyson

Horror fiction
H.P. Lovecraft's essay on the Supernatural
Stephen King's "Why Horror Movie's Scare Us"
a Poe horror story
a Lovecraft horror story
a contemporary horror story
a series of short clips from several horror movies

The concept of equality
"The Declaration of Independence"—Thomas Jefferson
"The Gettysburg Address"—Abraham Lincoln
"I Have a Dream"—Martin Luther King

Process Essay Questions for Paper #5

Remember, when you're writing the process essay . . .

- Do not answer the questions in a list, but in a response essay try to cover each idea.
- You may move the questions around as you see fit, so don't restrict yourself to the question-answer format.
- Be conscientious of your format (twelve-point Roman/New Times Roman, double-spaced, one-inch margins, etc.).

- Explain the organization of your argument. Refer to the flow chart handout.

- After reviewing your research and organizing your argument, what conclusion(s) did you reach?

- What one piece of advice (either from a peer-editor, the teacher or the writing center,) helped the most?

- What do you see as some strengths of this paper? Is there anything in this paper that seems weak to you?

Part Seven
Case Study of Yourself as a Writer

Of all the assignments, formal and informal, that you have written this semester, this last paper, the case study of yourself as a writer, is by far the most important because it summarizes all that you have learned in English 180 about writing, *your* writing, and about yourself as a writer. If you take nothing else away from this class, take this paper and keep it because it is your personal writing guide for future writing tasks in college and beyond. Here in this case study you look back on the other five papers you have written and examine all the drafts of those papers, the feedback you received from your teacher and your classmates, your own process sheets recording what you did when you wrote each paper, your error lists, and any source materials you used for any of those papers. In other words, now you are analyzing yourself as a writer—your strengths and weaknesses and your particular writing problems and your attempts to solve them by examining all your writing work this semester. Like Paper #2, your self-reflection that analyzed your own personal experience narrative, you will now reflect upon all the writing you did over the course of the semester to discover and record what you have learned about yourself as a writer.

Remember back in the beginning of this book when we told you that the goal of English 180 was to make you an effective, competent writer? Now you get to decide whether we succeeded or not. Paper #6 requires you to articulate for yourself, to yourself and your teacher, what you have learned about your writing and your writing processes this semester. Being able to articulate this knowledge proves that you are conscious of your own writing processes and can, therefore, control those processes in future courses to successfully complete any writing task. This awareness and control is really all we can teach you about future writing anyway. Knowing what you do well and what you need to still work on will enable you to continue to improve your writing for the rest of your life. We described this text as a kind of road map for successfully negotiating English 180. In the same vein, this case study is your own personal road map for successfully negotiating any future writing task, in school or out. Take this assignment seriously; it is *about* you, *for* you. Be honest and thorough; don't cheat yourself by throwing something together at the last minute. Go through the writing processes you have become aware of, use the synthesizing techniques you mastered earlier, and, by analyzing your own work in depth, produce the best paper you can write—for your teacher, certainly, but most of all, for yourself.

The Assignment Materials

This brief section deals with what you need for writing your case study. It includes the assignment sheet, the collection and review of materials process, and the peer review questions as well as a description of the in- and out-of-class activities that will help you to successfully complete this task.

All semester long we have reminded you to keep all your drafts for every assignment, including the final draft and the process sheet attached to it. "Throw everything in an expanding folder after you finish each assignment," your teacher said over and over. Well, now is the time to get out that folder and use those materials to complete your sixth and final assignment for English 180.

To begin, you need to locate the materials on this case study checklist and bring those materials to class for check-off day. This process ensures that you have all the necessary materials to write your case study:

Checklist of Materials for Paper #6: Case Study of Yourself as a Writer

Paper #1: Personal Narrative
- All rough drafts
- Teacher response draft
- Peer reviews
- Process questions and answers

Paper #2: Reflective Essay
- All rough drafts
- Teacher response draft
- Peer reviews
- Process questions and answers

Paper #3: Opinion Paper
- All rough drafts
- Teacher response draft
- Peer reviews
- Process questions and answers
- All sources used

Paper #4: Mini-Research Project
- All rough drafts
- Teacher response draft
- Peer reviews
- Process questions and answers
- All sources used

Paper #5: Essay Exam
- Teacher response graded draft
- Process questions and answers

and

Any other relevant material—journal entries or conference notes, for example—you feel will help you write this paper.

Next, we will devote a class to preparing you to actually write this assignment by going over the assignment sheet in class and then allowing you to freewrite answers to the eight questions on that sheet. These answers will generate the material that forms the basis of your paper by providing the specific details you need for writing your draft. The materials you have gathered from the previous step will provide you with any details or specifics you need when incorporating these answers into your paper.

Note that there are two possible ways to satisfy this assignment. You can choose to write in one of two different genres—the narrative or essay formats that you have already mastered in previous assignments. The questions you answer in class should prove equally helpful for either format. You should choose the one you like best and feel most comfortable with, the one that will allow you to write the best case study possible.

English 180
Assignment Six, The Case Study

Self Study of Yourself as a Writer

<u>Purpose of assignment</u>: Such a comprehensive process piece examining yourself as a writer this semester will enable both YOU and ME to assess what you have learned in this class. Even more important, expressing and organizing in writing the development of your own writing processes will help you to identify, control, and use those processes in future writing assignments.

<u>Requirements</u>: A four to six page paper with a title page containing your name, ID#, class and section, and the date. Paper must be double-spaced with standard one-inch margins. All rough drafts and teacher and peer feedback must also be included.

Steps for Writing a Self-Study of Your Own Writing Processes:

A. Assemble your semester portfolio. It should include five actual papers now:
   Personal narrative
   Self-reflection
   Controversial issue
   Mini-research paper
   Essay exam

   Also include process sheets for each paper, at least one rough draft per paper (except essay exam), and feedback from peers/teachers.

   In other words, you need everything you turned in with each paper and the paper itself, plus your error lists and any process journal entries not included with the actual papers.

B. Reread your process sheets and any separate process journal entries.

C. Freewrite on the following questions (we will do most of these in class and then discuss them in turn):
   1. What incidents do you remember from any of these writing assignments? What stands out in your mind about these writing experiences?

continues

English 180
Assignment Six, The Case Study (*Continued*)

2. Of all the assignments, which did you like best? Least? Why? OR, which was easiest to write? Hardest? Why?

3. Consider the physical aspects of your writing. When do you write? Where? How fast or how slow? Do you use a pen, pencil, computer?

4. How long is your usual writing session? How do you feel when you have finished?

5. Can you isolate elements of your writing process—generating ideas and creating a thesis, organizing material, writing a draft, rewriting, proofing and editing? Which is harder for you? Easier?

6. What role did response or feedback—peer and teacher—play in your writing process? How much/little did it affect your revision?

7. What specific problems did you encounter? (You may consider one particular paper here or the semester in general.) Were you ever stuck developing an idea or thesis in writing a draft? How did you solve that problem?

8. How do you feel about writing? Yourself as a writer? Has this changed over the course of the semester?

NOW:

D. Reread all your material, including the freewriting on these eight questions. You have now familiarized yourself with all the materials you need for your case study.

E. Remember that you can write this paper in one of two different genres: a temporal narrative tracing your development as a writer through the semester OR a conceptual essay focused on and organized around certain aspect(s) of your writing process or problems with your writing that you feel are particularly important to you as a writer (in this case, be sure to state *why* each of these aspects is important to you). Choose one.

F. Produce a rough draft for teacher/peer feedback in class.

G. Using that response, write your final draft.

To help you organize and write your own case study, we include here the titles of several essays on writing by professional authors that the class can read and discuss as well as two past successful student examples.

Professional possibilities:

"Mother Tongue" by Amy Tan
"From Silence to Words: Writing as Struggle" by Min-zhan Lu

Practice, Practice, Practice
Eddy L. Butler

Jeffrey A. Carver once said, "Practice, practice, practice writing. Writing is a craft that requires both talent and acquired skills. You learn by doing, by making mistakes and then seeing where you went wrong." While many people in class may have complained that the number of papers we were required to produce throughout the semester was almost overwhelming, it is now easy to see that we were just living through Carver's words. We were constantly practicing, not only in writing for this English class and for future English classes, but also in writing for other classes, our jobs, and our lives.

The first paper assigned in English 180 was the personal narrative. A friend of mine, a former 180 student, told me that this paper was the easiest to write because it was a mere transcript of something personal that had happened in our lives. We could choose anything we wanted, whether it was a recent event or something we had done as toddlers. However, I found that I had some difficulty writing this paper because it was tempting to write about two or three events instead of focusing just on one, and it was also hard to narrow down the time period to a day or less instead of months or even years. Some people expressed the same frustration about this problem of attaining focus, but in reflection, it was best to get it out of the way with the first paper. I had originally written about my Spring Break trip to Barbados, which took place over a week. Many small details were included—I had no problem with description—but I had tried to pack too much information into two pages. The instructor said that I should focus on one part of the trip, probably the day or event that I would recall most easily and clearly because it is most important to me. From there, I narrowed my decision down to the first day, which was significant because it was the first time I had ever left the U.S., and the day I was almost attacked by a shark. I then chose to focus on the shark story because I thought it was more interesting to read, and I found that it was easier to write about because I could incorporate a lot of feelings and clear mental images that haunt me until today. This practice of narrowing down the subject, from broad to narrow, really helped me to keep focus on my papers, and helped later, when I needed to specify an argument—in other words, write a thesis—for my opinion and research papers.

Having to narrow down my narrative even further to make it into a reflection paper was equally, if not more, challenging. For the reflection paper, we were asked to think about the subject of our narrative, and then think about its significance in a broader perspective. We were told to think of the lessons we learned from our experience, and how it has affected our lives. My teacher explained that we should be asking ourselves "why"—why it is important to me, why it would be important to other people, why it matters, why it takes precedence over other events. It was especially hard to write this paper because I usually don't analyze my actions. Through writing this paper, I now see details of my experience that I probably would never have given a second thought about in daily life. In addition, because I kept thinking of the "why" questions, I found that my ability to defend my argument grew stronger, which helped a lot in writing the opinion and research papers.

Next to defending arguments and focusing on a topic, the plain act of getting thoughts down on paper is something I found difficult. I feel like a lot of people have this problem: there are a lot of great ideas in our minds, but the ideas just don't seem right when we type or write them out. Because of this, I feel that freewriting played an important role in our development as writers. Without having to worry about structure or grammar and punctuation, we were allowed to simply let our ideas flow. Sometimes I felt like freewriting wasn't very different from what I wrote in my regular

continues

Practice, Practice, Practice (Continued)
Eddy L. Butler

papers because I felt like I was just creating word-vomit for my papers anyway. However, when I realized the advantage that freewriting gave me—something to work with instead of staring at a blank page—I also realized that my writing in papers were much more organized because of freewriting.

Thanks to freewriting, the in-class essay was not very difficult to write. Many people might say that the in-class essay is their least favorite paper assignment, but I disagree. It was actually my favorite because it was a research-style essay, which I feel confident writing, but we could stray from traditional research themes and choose to write about unique topics like fairytales. We were provided with a theme and texts to read (one was a film) by our teacher, but we decided on possible essay questions as a class, which I really liked because it didn't feel so "institutional." After hearing that many people write their papers at the last minute, I thought that the 50-minute time period we were allowed to write the essay in was not such a bad deal. It was almost like free-writing in the sense that we had to jot down what we knew about a subject in a fairly small amount of time, except we also needed to self-edit our essays to see if the organization worked, if the paper flowed well, and whether or not our transitions and back-up arguments made sense. But, with the ability to funnel my knowledge on the topic and just get my ideas down really helped because I actually had something to work with, to rearrange and edit to make a "good essay."

While I think I need to work harder on my transitions between paragraphs and sentences in papers, I think that I have improved a lot over the course of writing the 5 papers. I've learned that you can't just throw in a quote without something to explain what the significance of that quote is. The fact that you are quoting something probably means that it is significant, but again, you have to answer "why" it's so great. From working on transitions between "narrative" and "reflection" in the second paper, to "private" and "public" writing in freewrites, to opinion and research in the third and fourth papers, I'm glad to have practiced working with transitions in my writing.

As I mentioned, I've had problems with transitions, but in a way, writing is all about transitions—moving from one stepping-stone to another. I look forward to my transition from English 180 to 280, and whatever the next step is for me as a writer in my career and in my life. Someone once told me, "practice makes perfect, but only you can define what perfection is." Just as stated in Carver's quote, "practice, practice, practice" is what I have taken from this class, and though I am far from perfection as a writer, at least I now know what I am looking for and what goals to set for myself.

Changes
Michael Crane

When I started my 180 class this semester, I was really hesitant. I thought it would be a waste of my time. I wrote in high school, so I knew how to write papers. This class is for people who didn't know what they were doing. That's what I thought. I thought that my writing wouldn't improve. I'd just write the papers—the night before they were due—and I'd get at least a B in the class.

I was very much mistaken. For one thing, I couldn't write papers the night before they were due. Since I had to have peers respond to the paper, I had to write a rough draft. Still, when I first heard this, I figured I would just reprint the rough draft. I've had other students look at my stuff before, in high school, and they never gave me any advice that helped. They just said that things were great, that it was really clear, and that it was a great paper. If that was the only kind of advice I was going to get, then there wasn't a point in writing two drafts.

But the questions we were given didn't allow those kinds of answers. The people who looked at my stuff gave me real advice, things that I could actually respond to and things that I could actually fix. When I went back and fixed my draft because of all their advice, I found that my second draft was a whole lot better. I felt like I actually earned the grade, like I actually worked for it.

When I started writing this paper, I went back through all my other assignments. I looked at the free writes we did on the first day of class, then I looked at the one I did towards the end of the semester. I looked at my first paper and compared it to my fifth. Well, I wasn't all that surprised that the free write was so much better. I'd been writing free writes three times a week all semester; of course they'd get better. But what really surprised me was that paper five was so much better than paper one. I mean, I wrote paper one at home, where I was relaxed, and I took my time with it. Paper five was an in class essay. I had to write the entire thing in fifty minutes, and I only had one page of notes to help me do it. But it was still better than my first one. I guess my writing really has improved over the semester.

I guess it all comes to the things that I learned in this class. I learned that if I write a draft and give it a few days, I can find a whole bunch of things to improve. And if I give it to someone with real guidelines for what I'm looking for, they can give me the kind of advice that I need to make a better paper. And it's so much better writing multiple drafts. I write at least three drafts for all my papers now, and I get nothing but A's, even in my other classes.

I also learned that if you write a lot, you get better. My instructor kept saying that writing was like a muscle, but I didn't understand what he was saying. It's true though. The more you write, the better you get, and the easier it gets to do. It took me about five hours to write my first paper, and it was only three pages long! By the time I wrote the research paper, I didn't need nearly that much time. I mean, I needed time to do the research and all that, but we did that along the way. When I actually sat down and wrote it, I knocked out six pages in about two hours. That's so much faster than I used to be!

continues

Changes (*Continued*)
Michael Crane

Also, page length gets to be less and less of a problem. When I was in high school, a five page paper was a major project. It was a big deal that I needed at least a month to do. Most stuff was just a page or two. When I found out I'd have to write papers that were four to six pages more than once in a semester, I was really scared. I almost dropped the course. I probably would have if it weren't a requirement. But I didn't, and I'm glad I didn't. Now five pages is nothing to me. I'm still a little intimidated knowing that I'll have to write papers ten to fifteen pages long, but I feel confident that I can learn how. Sooner or later, that'll be just as easy as writing four pages is now.

I also learned that what I thought was the best way to write wasn't. I used to think that the way to write a paper was to shut off all the music, get away from all distractions, and force yourself to pump the whole thing out all at once. I always wanted to write it first by hand, because I thought that would help, but I never managed that. I thought that was the way to do it, though. At the start of the semester, when I was told I could write however I wanted, I thought it was a trick. I thought it meant however I wanted, so long as it was the way the teacher wanted.

Then, when I had to write paper two, I didn't have time to go to the library. It was raining out and I didn't feel like walking through that. So I just sat down with my laptop in my room. My roommate was listening to music, and I didn't feel like fighting, so I didn't say anything. I just sat there, facing the wall and listening to music. That was so much easier than sitting in the library. I felt secluded, but I was also relaxed. I learned that you really can write however you want to. Now I write my papers with an iPod on. I still prefer to write alone, but it's not as big a deal. And I don't write all in one sitting anymore.

When I wrote the third paper, I wrote it all in one sitting. And I noticed that about halfway through, it started to suck. My instructor noticed that too, but he said it much more nicely. He suggested that when I start feeling tired, I should stop writing. Do something else for a while, he said. Come back to it. So that's what I did for my rewrite, and it was so much better. Now I write about two or three pages at a time, then go for a jog to think about things. When I come back, then I write the rest. It works out really well.

I thought this class would be a waste of my time. I'm so glad I didn't act on that. I could have just coasted, not tried, and gotten a C. I could have convinced myself that I wouldn't gain anything, that my instructor couldn't teach me anything. But I didn't. I took things seriously, and I really tried. I'm glad I did. If I hadn't done that, I don't think I would've gotten the A I'm pretty sure I'm going to get. And I definitely wouldn't have gotten an A in my political science class, because that was all papers too. I feel pretty confident about my writing now, and I'm almost looking forward to 280. How much more can I learn? I don't know. But I didn't think I could learn anything at the start of this semester, and look how wrong I was about that. Next time I'm going into it with the idea that I can learn a whole lot. That way, maybe I'll get even more out of that class than I did out of this one.

The third class devoted to this assignment will be peer workshopping of your draft. The process for workshopping the narrative and the essay are the same, but the specific questions differ for each choice. If you are responding to a narrative for a fellow student, use those seven narrative questions. If you are responding to an essay, use the eight essay questions.

Peer Feedback for Paper #6, Self Study of Yourself as a Writer

This is your final paper of the semester. Hopefully it will demonstrate your improvement as a writer as well as your ability to recognize and correct problems with your content, organization, style, diction, and mechanics. Take time today to get feedback from your fellow students and your teacher; make this the best piece of writing you are capable of producing. Write a very brief note to your editors, asking them to check for specific problems.

- Pass your paper to your left.
- In turn, each editor (not the writer) reads aloud the paper he/she has just received.
- Stop if anyone in the group "hears" an error and give the writer (with the group's help) a chance to correct it.
- Now begin written feedback. Each "editor/responder" should answer the following questions either on this sheet or on the text of the paper. If answered on the paper, write "on paper" on this sheet.
- Locate the thesis and underline it. Then answer either the set A or set B questions after you have decided whether the paper is a **narrative** or an **essay**.

If a **narrative**:

1. Does it cover multiple papers throughout the semester or the producing of one or two specific papers?
2. Is it organized chronologically? Is that order logical? Is anything out of place? Is anything left out? Should anything be added?
3. Does the conclusion follow naturally? Does it fit? Is it complete? If not, what needs to be added? Is it repetitious? If so, what needs to be eliminated?
4. Reread the introduction. Does it capture your interest? Would you want to read this paper? Why? What in this intro "hooks" you? Be specific. Suggest improvements if the intro doesn't "hook" you.
5. Circle your favorite passage in the text. Discuss what you like about it.
6. Box in a problem section, one that is weak or confusing, one that needs to be rewritten for some reason. State the problem with the passage here. Suggest ways to improve it.
7. What kind of grade would you give this paper? Why?

If an **essay**:

1. Identify the problem(s) or part of the writing process the student is discussing. State it in one sentence.
2. Does the paper stay on track, stay focused on this problem (problems) or process?
3. Number in the paper the individual points the student uses to discuss his or her problem or process. How many are there? Should there be more? Are any repetitious? Should any be eliminated?
4. Is the conclusion logical? Complete? Could it be improved? In what ways?
5. Does the intro catch your attention? What "hooks" you? Be specific. Suggest improvements if the intro doesn't "hook" you.
6. Circle your favorite passage. Discuss what you like about it.
7. Box off the weakest passage and suggest ways to improve it.
8. What kind of grade would you give this paper? Why?

Hopefully, there will be time to share some special segments of your case studies with your classmates when we meet during final exam week.

Appendix

Writer's Block and Solutions
Portfolios
Top Ten Errors

Writer's Block and Solutions

All writers, from those just starting out to professional authors, experience writer's block from time to time. Fortunately, there are several ways writers can break through this barrier. All of the following invention activities have been used in English classrooms for a number of years and have proven themselves useful to writers of all skill levels. Try one or all of these invention exercises when writer's block strikes.

Freewriting

When you are struggling to find topics to write on or have too many ideas and are not sure where to begin, grab a sheet of paper and a pencil and begin writing whatever it is that is on your mind for at least a period of ten minutes. Do not stop even if you feel you have nothing to write about. Just keep going. When ten minutes are up, review what you have written for topics.

Breaking It Down

When you receive a writing assignment, break the topic down into different levels and brainstorm on a single item.

- General Topic: Capital Punishment
- Possible Subtopics/Questions: Should the court system be allowed to sentence minors to death row?
- Repetitive terms or phrases: Sometimes writers repeat words or phrases too many times. Brainstorm for possible variations in order to add variety to your paper.

Listing or Bulleting

When you have a broad topic that you want to make more specific, try formulating a list of possible subtopics under your general one:

<u>Environmental Issues</u>

Global Warming	Water Contamination	Limited Energy Resources
Green House Gas	Soil Quality	Wind Power
City Bicycle Programs	Animal Rights	Solar Energy
Sierra Club	Recycling	Resource Conservation
Transportation	"Green" Construction	Coal Mining
Hybrid Vehicles	Economic effects	Local/Organic Food
Movements		

Cubing

When you are struggling to find an approach to a topic, use cubing as a brainstorming strategy. Cubing allows you to rethink your topic from six different approaches.

1. Describe your topic.
2. Compare it.
3. Associate it.
4. Analyze it.
5. Apply it.
6. Argue for and against it.

Review your answers for any new suggestions about your topic. Are there any patterns or themes that exist among your responses? Does one response seem particularly interesting to you? Do you think you could formulate a thesis statement from one of these approaches?

Clustering/Mapping/Webbing

On a large sheet of paper or on the blackboard, write your general topic in the center. Then, branching out from the center as if creating a web, write down as many related concepts or terms as you can think of. From those concepts or terms, continue to write down related ideas. If you can't think of things that are similar, write down opposites, associations, or anything you can think of in order to keep your brain and hands moving.

When you are finished jotting down ideas, take a step back and begin circling ideas that seem related and draw lines connecting the circles. When you run out of terms that relate, choose another word and begin making connections. When you are finished, you should have a series of webs that you can begin to develop conclusions about how to approach a topic.

Journalistic Questions

Ask yourself the "big six" journalistic questions: Who? What?, When?, Where?, Why?, and How?. Write these words on a piece of paper leaving plenty of room for responses. Then, answer each question fully. Take a look at your responses. What questions were you able to elaborate more on? Was there a question you have no answer to? Do you think you can formulate a thesis from the information that you have gathered?

Purpose and Audience

- When you are struggling to find the "so what" of your paper, ask yourself the following questions: What is your purpose? What are you trying to do? What verb captures your intent? Are you trying to inform? Convince? Describe?
- Who is your audience? Who are you writing to other than your teacher? What information does your audience need to know? What do they already know?

Similes

Complete the following:

_____ is/was/are/were like _____.

Enter one of the terms or concepts that your paper centers on in the first blank. Then, brainstorm as many answers as possible for the second blank. After you have created a list of ideas, think about patterns or associations that appear.

Poetry   a painting

_____ is/was/are/were like _____.

Charting

If you are more visually inclined, it may help to create a chart to organize your ideas. Draw a table with different headings or subtopics and brainstorm words or ideas that relate to those subjects.

Conclusion

Remember, every writer experiences writer's block; however, there are remedies that you can test in order to overcome it. These are merely a few of the multiple invention exercises that are used in English classrooms, and you will most likely find that some work better for you than others given your point in the writing process and your overall assignment. Give each of these examples a try so that writer's block doesn't prevent you from writing wonderful papers.

Portfolios: What? Why? When? How?

The Rationale:

First and foremost, portfolios provide an assessment check on all English 180 sections. Since two instructors—your teacher who is familiar with your writing and your writing processes and another teacher who does not know you at all—have to agree that your writing passes or fails English 180's exit standards, the Writing Program is ensuring that all students satisfying this graduation requirement have reached at least a minimum college writing competency. Thus, and most important of all, the portfolio replaces the need for any kind of objective exit test in grammar and mechanics so prevalent, and so pointless, in measuring writing competency, in other colleges and universities.

Second, the portfolio system gives you the student the chance to be evaluated, not on one genre of writing—as exit essay exams often do—but on three different genres that you choose to submit for the portfolio. You get to pick your best writing for this evaluation. Different students excel in different types of writing; to evaluate any single student's writing ability on one paper alone is unfair because it could be your weakest genre and would not be a fair representation of your writing abilities. In the portfolio system you can choose among four genres: narrative, reflection, argumentative, and analytical. And, if you are a weak writer in one of the three areas you choose, strong papers in the other two will carry the portfolio to a pass. Your writing is evaluated on the portfolio as a whole, not on the individual papers.

Third, all good writing is rewriting. The portfolio system gives you the opportunity to be judged on your best writing because the pieces that you have chosen will be revised several times, using both peer and teacher feedback to produce the best possible papers you are capable of writing, before you submit them for evaluation. The portfolio resolves the process/product dilemma that composition studies has always debated because the objective reader can only evaluate the product, thus ensuring that the products the students produce in the future will meet the standards expected from university writing assignments; but the other reader, your teacher, knows you and saw your writing processes in operation and can add that knowledge to the evaluative equation.

Finally, the portfolio, from your point of view, requires very little additional work when compared to studying for an objective exit exam or preparing to write a timed final essay exam in class. For the portfolio, all you need to do is follow the feedback on your final graded paper, rewrite and reorganize where necessary, delete material you don't need, add material you do need, and correct grammatical and mechanical errors. Since all your drafts are on computers, this final revision of each paper submitted should not take very much time at all.

The Process:

The portfolio process consists of two different readings, a dry run held at midterm and a final reading in the last week of the semester.

The Dry Run

For the dry run each of you will choose one of the two or three papers that you have completed and that has received both peer and teacher feedback and/or graded commentary. Your choice should then be rewritten, using that feedback to create the best paper you are capable of writing at that point in the semester. A clean copy of that rewritten paper (one with no comments or grades on it) must be turned in to your instructors early enough for them to have time to check through the submissions to ensure all have section numbers and cover sheets and all are the students' own work, that they are the papers they, the teachers, have already graded and responded to. When teachers submit papers for the reading, they are certifying that those papers are the ones their students wrote. Plagiarism is not an issue in these readings unless readers discover two or more identical papers during the readings.

For each paper, you will write a cover sheet that contains the following information, not necessarily in that order:

- Identification of the genre of the paper turned in (narrative, reflection, etc.)
- Reason you chose that paper to turn in for the dry run
- A statement of your purpose in writing that paper (to tell a story, describe a person or event, reflect upon and analyze a personal experience, present an opinion on a controversial issue, etc.)

- A brief account of the actual process of writing and rewriting the paper (the number of drafts, additions or deletions to the content, reorganization, help from others, etc.)
- Any other relevant information you or the teacher thinks may help an unknown reader to accurately evaluate the paper.

For the dry run standards are slightly higher than the final passing criteria because there is still time for you to improve the papers and because instructors want to make certain that all borderline papers, in the low to mid C range, are rewritten before the final reading to strengthen the overall portfolio so that you will pass the course. Those of you who fail the dry run will be given a failure sheet listing the errors and stating what you must do to make the failed paper into a passing one. This grade is not recorded anywhere. It simply means that your writing has not yet reached the passing level for college standards, but you get another chance to revise, using yet another set of professional feedback from a teacher not your own. Those of you who pass receive a "P" on your papers. Those passes are recorded by your teacher, and you resubmit that paper, along with two more of your choice, for the final reading at the end of the semester. In that reading the "P" paper does not have to be reread but, if one of the other two is weak, it will be rechecked to see if it is strong enough for the whole portfolio to pass.

The Final Portfolio

You choose your three best papers to turn in. If one has already passed the dry run, you should be sure that it is one of the three you turn in. All papers should be final, clean drafts—no teacher comments or grades and no peer responses. You do not turn in rough drafts or notes or any other preparatory materials. There should be a single cover letter for the portfolio that identifies all three papers and gives your rationale for choosing each one. It can also include any information you think the unknown reader needs to know to judge the papers fairly. The cover letter can be in essay form, letter format, or any other appropriate genre. Each paper should be stapled, not paper clipped, and all the pages of each should be numbered. The three papers should be placed in your manila envelope in the order that they were assigned in the class, earliest first. This is also the order in which they should be discussed in the cover letter.

In the final reading, two readers must certify that you are writing at a C or higher level for you to pass English 180. One reader is your teacher, and the other is the unknown portfolio reader, also an English 180 teacher but one who does not know you at all. The two readers must agree on the pass or fail evaluation or a third reader will be brought in to resolve the stalemate. It is possible to pass the portfolio and still fail the course for other reasons (absences, other grades that drop the overall grade below a C average, plagiarism, etc.). If you fail the portfolio, however, you cannot pass English 180. Less than 10 percent of English 180 students fail the course, and most of those fail for absences and/or missing work. In other words, it isn't that they can't do the work; they don't do the work.

It is also possible for a portfolio to pass with one paper that needs mechanical surface cleanup—minor punctuation errors, misspellings, etc. The outside reader must state that situation on the failure sheet, and the teacher must see the corrected paper before turning in a passing grade for the student for the course. Remember that this is a portfolio; we are judging all the papers as a whole unit. Therefore, one could be a failing paper, but, if the other two are strong enough to pull the portfolio up to a passing level, the portfolio passes. In the dry run we fail anything below a solid C because you have time to improve the paper and we feel that you will learn something about your own writing in the process. Now the rules have changed for the final reading. Any paper that is a C– or better passes. That's the minimum for English 180 competence, but it is still competence. The question is, are you writing at a level that you can go on to English 280; or, put another way, do you need to repeat English 180?

If your teacher disagrees with the outside reader's pass or fail, your teacher must submit that portfolio to a third reader for reconsideration. No teacher can change a portfolio grade. He or she must find another teacher whose reading agrees with his or hers. The whole purpose of portfolios is to ensure that two qualified teachers, one who knows the student and one who does not, agree on the final pass/fail portfolio status.

The Ten Top Problems for Freshman Writers at WIU

To compile this list, the Director of Writing polled the WIU Writing Faculty to determine the most frequently found writing problems and errors in first year writing students' papers. This is not a ranked list, just a compilation of the results of that poll in no particular order. We include it here for you so that, if you have one or more of these problems in your writing, you will be able to recognize the problem right away and know where in the Hacker handbook to go for help. The list will also aid you in identifying your writing problems when you go to the Writing Center for tutoring help with any of your formal paper assignments.

1. Comma splices—a punctuation issue that arises when you incorrectly insert a comma between two independent clauses (complete sentences that could stand alone) instead of the period or semicolon that you need in this construction. You can also correct this problem by adding a coordinate conjunction after the existing comma.

Example:

Incorrect:
The fire raged throughout the night, four neighborhood houses burned to the ground.

Correct:
<u>With a period</u>: The fire raged throughout the night. Four neighborhood houses burned to the ground.
<u>With a semicolon</u>: The fire raged throughout the night; four neighborhood houses burned to the ground.
<u>With the addition of a coordinating conjunction</u>: The fire raged throughout the night, and four neighborhood houses burned to the ground.

2. Fused or run-on sentences: Closely related to the comma splice, this is an error that occurs when two or more sentences run together with no intervening punctuation. This problem can be corrected by inserting a period, a semicolon, or a comma and a coordinate conjunction in the proper space between the separate complete sentences.

Example:

Incorrect: The police pursued the bear he escaped into the woods.

Correct:
<u>With a period</u>: The police pursued the bear. He escaped into the woods.

<u>With a semicolon</u>: The police pursued the bear; he escaped into the woods.
<u>With a comma and conjunction</u>: The police pursued the bear, but he escaped into the woods.
<u>Or you can rewrite the sentence to reflect the sequential order or logical relationship involved</u>—When the police pursued the bear, he escaped into the woods.

3. Fragments: A sentence structural problem that occurs when you write an incomplete thought as a whole sentence. A fragment could be just a phrase without a subject and verb—"None of the above." Or it could be a dependent clause with a subject and a verb but one unable to make sense unless it is attached to an independent clause—"while I was waiting for you."

Example:

Incorrect: None of the above

Correct:
<u>Adding a necessary verb</u>: None of the above were finished on time.

Incorrect:
While I was waiting for you

Correct:
<u>Attached to an independent clause</u>: While I was waiting for you, I sat in the nearby park and read a book.

4. Unnecessary repetition: This problem splits into two categories:

    (1) The repetition of single words throughout a paper. For example, the use of the word *shoppers* twenty times in a two page description of people at a mall. Here you need to either use a replacement word meaning the same thing, like *customers* or *consumers*, or, when appropriate, a pronoun like "they" or "them," depending on whether the need is for a subjective or objective case.

    (2) The unnecessary repetition of the same idea or point that you have already made in a paper. Here you merely state the same point you have already made in different words. This problem occurs frequently in beginning writers' texts because they have not yet learned to fully develop their ideas and instead, in order to meet the required number of pages, they repeat what they have already written, using slightly different phrasing. The way to solve this problem is to learn how to logically and fully develop each point or idea in your paper so that you will have no problem meeting the length requirement.

5. Wordiness: When making this stylistic error, students use far more words than they need to make a statement. This error can take many forms, but one of the most frequent is the use of passive rather than active voice in paper assignments. For example, "The soccer bus was driven by Ronnie's mother."

This is a passive construction that requires eight words. The rewrite to active voice, "Ronnie's mother drove the soccer bus," requires only six words. Again, passive constructions allow the student to fill more space but are less direct and are not effective writing. All passive constructions that can be rewritten into active voice should be.

Another frequent wordiness problem is redundancies. For example, "Jennie is employed at a computer firm working as a software engineer."

All you need here is a condensed version that retains exactly the same meaning: "Jennie works at a computer firm as a software engineer."

The problem of wordiness means that the student is, consciously or unconsciously, padding a text without really developing ideas and points fully. Reducing that padding forces a writer to develop those ideas and points to fulfill the page requirement.

6. Pronoun References: This error always occurs when a reader cannot trace the pronoun directly back to its antecedent (the noun to which the pronoun refers). In some cases, the antecedent is too far away from the pronoun because the antecedent must be in the same paragraph as the pronoun to be directly connected to it. In other cases, the antecedent is unclear. There is more than one noun to which the pronoun could refer, and the reader cannot tell which is the right one. And finally, the pronoun may have no antecedent, and, in that situation, the reader has no idea to whom the pronoun refers. All three are serious errors because they can cause a reader to misread and therefore misunderstand a writer's meaning.

7. Dangling modifier: This error occurs when the modifier (usually an adjective or an adverb) does not connect logically to any other word in the sentence. For example,

"Getting out of the car, the parking lot was filled with snow."

We all know a parking lot cannot get out of a car, so who got out? Because there is no noun or pronoun for the phrase to connect with, it is "dangling."

There are several ways to rewrite this incorrect sentence:

(1)   Getting out of the car, she found the parking lot filled with snow.

This solution provides a pronoun, in this case "she," for the modifying phrase to connect with.

(2)   When she got out of the car, the parking lot was full of snow.

This second solution eliminates the dangling phrase altogether without changing the meaning of the sentence.

8. Failure to balance parallel items: Parallelism means that, if two or more concepts or ideas or objects are of equal or parallel value, they should be expressed in parallel grammatical form.

    You can have a list of nouns, a list of phrases, a list of clauses or a list of sentences, but do not mix the forms in a single listing. For example:

    "Children who study karate also develop coordination, fitness, and they are confident."

    This is incorrect because you have two nouns (coordination and fitness) and a sentence (they are confident) listed in a series. The correct structure would be a list of three nouns:

    "Children who study karate also develop coordination, fitness and confidence."

9. Incorrect diction choices: While students have always had issues choosing the wrong word for a particular phrase or sentence, the arrival of computer technology has compounded this original problem because spell check often misreads your incorrect spelling and substitutes a word totally different in meaning from the one you originally intended.

    For example, the number one error in the category for beginning writers at Western is the spell check substitution of the word *defiantly* for the word *definitely*. Obviously students' misspellings of the word are closer to "defiantly" than "definitely," and spell check, which cannot read context at all, chooses the word it thinks the student is trying to spell. Since students cannot spell the word in the first place, they never catch the error when proofreading their own papers. This is a problem that must be caught by another reader.

10. Misplaced modifiers: This is an error of placement within a sentence. Here the modifier is placed too far away from the word or phrase that it modifies and too near another word that it appears to modify but does not. This is a serious error because it may interfere with the meaning of the sentence. For example,

    "The police officer directed traffic with a head cold."

    The modifying phrase, "with a head cold" is syntactically connected to the traffic, not the police officer. Common sense tells us that people, not traffic, get colds; therefore the phrase, "with a head cold," needs to be moved closer to officer and away from traffic. The corrected version should read:

    "The police officer with a head cold directed traffic."

    In this case, the error is easily corrected, but in more complicated constructions, it may be more difficult for a reader to decode the writer's meaning and move the misplaced modifier next to the word it was intended to modify. In these instances, only the writers can clarify meaning by moving the phrase because only they know what it was intended to describe in the first place. All a reader can do is to point out the confusion and ask the writer to clarify the meaning.